FAMILIES IN TRANSITION

FAMILIES IN TRANSITION
Divorce, Remarriage and the Stepfamily

Don Martin
Maggie Martin
Western Illinois University

Sheffield Publishing Company
Salem, Wisconsin

For information about this book, write or call:

Sheffield Publishing Company
P.O. Box 359
Salem, Wisconsin 53168
(414) 843-3802

Copyright © 1985 by Don Martin and Maggie Martin
ISBN 0-88133-179-1

All rights reserved. No part of this book may be reproduced, stored in a retrieval system, or transmitted in any form or by any means without permission in writing from the publisher.

Printed in the United States of America.

Dr. Don Martin and Dr. Maggie Martin are affiliated with Western Illinois University, College of Education, Counselor Education and College Student Personnel, Macomb, Illinois, 61455.

To our children, Paige, Sean and Erin, with love and hope for the future

PREFACE

This book was developed for individuals who are contemplating beginning a stepfamily or those who are already a member of this type of family unit. It is based on our own experiences as a stepfamily and the many families we have counseled and attempted to help.

When we began facing difficulties in our own family, it soon became evident to us that there was limited material for us to read concerning stepfamilies. Either these books were too technical or they were written by individuals who lived in families but had little counseling experience. Even when we did find books that seemed appropriate, we found ourselves disagreeing with the author's basic philosophy that stepfamilies could never be normal. They appeared doomed to a life of unhappiness and constant struggle where it takes years to understand family members and that only "time" eventually healed all wounds.

In contrast to this viewpoint, we believed that stepfamilies could be happy and seemed to have as good a chance at expressing healthy behaviors as other types of families. In our counseling sessions, we found that many stepfamily members cared deeply for each other and seemed blocked as how to get past family barriers so that they could be free to love, respect, and communicate with each family member. It is in this regard that we began to formulate writing a book that could express our own thoughts on how we helped stepfamilies. This book is a culmination of all those experiences and we believe it provides an effective model for stepfamilies that seem more satisfactory ways of living.

Acknowledgements

There are many people that have been an inspiration to us and very helpful in the development of our ideas. We are particularly grateful to all the families we have counseled and their willingness to let us into their private worlds. Others participated in several research projects and, to these families we are also grateful.

Since our jobs have entailed providing counseling and the training of future therapists, we wish to thank all of our graduate students at Northeastern Oklahoma State University, New Mexico State University, and Western Illinois University. Their ideas have always been challenging to us and they have helped us develop our theories.

We are indebted to our colleagues in particular to Byron Medler at North Texas State University for his consistent love and encouragement. To Don Waterstreet and Dave Taylor and our other colleagues at Western Illinois University. We give a warm thanks for providing a nurturing environment where our creativity could flourish. To Becky May, who has always professionally met our demanding timetable without complaint a sincere thank you. A sincere thank you to Neil Rowe and Steve Nelson who were very supporting and encouraging of this project. And lastly to Norma, Harley and Jim; your love is a reminder of our past and our path to the future.

Macomb, Illinois										Don and Maggie Martin
April, 1985

THE AUTHORS

Don Martin: received his Ph.D. in Counseling from North Texas State University. He is a faculty member in the department of Counselor Education at Western Illinois University in Macomb, Illinois. Dr. Marting is a licensed psychologist and an approved supervisor in the American Association for Marriage and Family Therapy.

He has published numerous articles in psychological and educational journals. In addition, Dr. Martin has presented workshops both regionally and nationally on remarriage and stepfamily counseling. He maintains a private practice specializing in couple and family therapy.

Maggie Martin: received her Ed.D. in Counseling Psychology from the University of Tulsa. She is a counseling psychologist in the counseling Center and an adjunct faculty member in the department of Counselor Education at Western Illinois University in Macomb, Illinois. Dr. Martin is a member of the American Pyschological Association and the American Association of Marriage and Family Therapy.

Because of her experience in public schools and child guidance centers, Dr. Martin has been a consultant to teachers and mental health counselors who work with children from stepfamilies. She has published numerous articles in professional journals and has presented national workshops on remarriage and stepfamily counseling. In addition, she maintains a private practice in marriage and family therapy.

CONTENTS

Preface		vii
Authors		x
Chapters:		
1	Understanding the Stepfamily	1
2	Coping with Divorce	9
3	Beginning New Relationships	23
4	Money from Divorce	37
5	The Role of Children When Deciding to Remarry	50
6	The Effects of the Ex-spouse on Remarriage	65
7	Integrating the Family	78
8	Establishing a Stepfamily Lifestyle	92
9	Old Memories and the Stepfamily	105
10	The Role of the Custodial Parent	118
11	Dilemmas of the Step Parent	132
12	Preventing Friction in the Stepfamily	145
13	Creating a Family Atmosphere	157
14	Understanding Children's Behavior in the Stepfamily	170
15	The Effects of Relatives, Professionals, and Society on the Stepfamily	189
16	Creating Your Own Future, in the Future	204

Understanding the Stepfamily

Families are changing! Children in school classrooms, close friends, and relatives all show the effects of the changing family in our culture. Professionals call this type of family--the stepfamily. It is a family where one parent is a stepparent and the children may live full time in the family or visit frequently or infrequently.

The stepfamily has not yet received its due approval but it will. Each of us may not have a choice in this matter, since the stepfamily appears to be the most growing type of family in our society. At present rates, this means that in the near future, the stepfamily may replace the traditional family as the dominant form of family in America.

Yet the stepfamily is rarely accepted by American society. There are no cultural norms, no rules, and no models for this type of family and its existence has been virtually ignored.

Today in America, approximately 15 percent of American families have one parent who is not biological related to the children. Over 15 million children and approximately 25 million adult parents live in stepfamilies. At this present rate, one million children and half a million adults each year become members of stepfamilies. Combine this with recent estimates that one out of two first marriages and 40 percent of second marriages end in divorce and one begins to realize the tremendous impact the stepfamily is having on our culture.

Having worked with stepfamilies for many years, we believe that individuals are concerned about how to help their families and reduce some of the difficulties stepfamilies face.

Parents want their children to grow up to be independent and emotionally healthy. However, the stepfamily faces hurdles that are different from those of traditional families. Some of these include:

1. <u>Stepfamily members have suffered the loss of an intimate relationship</u>. Whether through divorce or death, children and adults need to mourn and move beyond this loss. While this makes sense, it is not so easy to do. Coming to grips with saying goodbye or changing the structure of an intimate relationship causes severe strains on most families. Stepfamily members often blame themselves, and sometimes parents, for their difficulties. It's not unusual for a parent to have difficulty separating from an ex-spouse, whether physically, emotionally, or psychologically. This type of relationship may be even encouraged by the ex-spouse, who may or may not be remarried and desires attention or wishes to keep old ties.

Usually, this causes jealousy in the new spouse and all parties involved may end up in arguments. One spouse typically feels stuck in the middle as he or she ends up trying to please everybody. Pleasing the ex-spouse may be caused by guilt feelings and the realization that life will never be the same for the person who is alone. If individuals believe that they have disrupted the lives of their children, the guilt may be even more persuasive.

In stepfamilies, children will have some difficult adjustments. They may have feelings of hurt and loss, and unlike adults, expression of these feelings may be difficult. Instead of feeling sad, children may get very angry and displace their frustrations on to a stepparent. Sometimes simple situations will cause many memories to be awakened and this may prove painful.

2. <u>Old traditions are preserved but new traditions must be created for the stepfamily</u>. Stepfamily members have memories of the past when they begin the family. They have been in a family before and thus have some expectations.

While part of the past is necessary for a family to maintain continuity, focusing too much on old traditions can cause problems. Developing customs and common experiences help families get closer. Talking about common memories leaves a bond between members even if these experiences have been difficult.

Some of the more common problems arising from the past are these:

- A. Problems with discipline can arise between the spouse and the new parent. The children may not listen to the new parent or else this person may not wish to be involved or assume a parental role. The ex-spouse may also have difficulty with the involvement of the new parent or wish to play a significant part in the child's everyday affairs.

- B. New ways of behaving will be learned. Old rituals regarding eating, dressing, room cleaning, etc., may be questionable. The new parent and the biological parent may wish things to change because of past problems or due to the fact that these behaviors remind him or her of the ex-spouse. The children may be resistant to this and want things to be "as they were." Sometimes the biological parent may have felt inadequate as a parent and wants the new parent to be the leader. The kids can sense this and usually do not like things to straighten out. They may even try to complain or bring in the ex-spouse as a savior and complain about the step-parent.

- C. There will be great changes that nobody anticipates. If there is one thing that you can expect to happen in a stepfamily, it is that nothing will go smoothly for very long.

We recall one new parent we counseled who would have the same dream over and over again. In the dream he would be smiling and having a good time. Suddenly everyone would disappear or he would start to think of sad experiences. He felt his family was the same as his dream. Sometimes he feared that they would all leave him and he would be all alone with no one to love. Other times, he thought he could get close to the kids or to his wife and then suddenly it would change.

Stepfamilies have a very erratic beginning and seem to experience a "roller coaster" effect. Some typical examples of unexpected experiences that stepfamilies face are

- an ex-spouse who wants to renegotiate custody
- children who leave to live with the ex-spouse
- a non-custodial father who moves 2,000 miles to another city
- child-custody support abruptly ends
- a teenager runs away from home because of a disagreement with a new parent.

While these are just a small sampling of what can occur, many stepfamilies feel they have to deal with more stress than is typical in traditional families. Along with this, any type of emotional or psychological help is usually absent from the community or relatives. Many traditional families feel alone in their struggles but this is even more intense in the stepfamily.

D. Needs and expectations of family members may greatly differ. For instance, the children may not want the new parent to parent at all, while the new parent wants to be involved, or vice versa. Spouses in a stepfamily often have confusing expectations for each other because they are not sure of what to do in the stepfamily because of previous failures. A prevalent attitude in second marriages is "I'll never let you take advantage of me like my first spouse did!" So, everyone treads softly making sure no toes get stepped on.

E. Money, money, and more money--just like everyone else, stepfamilies fight over and worry about finances. Typical money problems focus around issues such as

- a new parent refusing to support the children
- resentment over custody money
- dual careers and how the incomes are shaped
- separate money for two families even though there is just one family
- resentment because an ex-spouse may become a "sugar-parent" and give the kids every conceivable material object they ever wanted

- comparisons between how great it was "back then" and how poor we are now.

Money is a tough issue to solve and generally if a stepfamily is of a higher economic status its problems are decreased. We don't believe money is less important to traditional families but rather that money issues are often more easy to argue about in stepfamilies because of the different types of people involved in the family, particularly because of the power of outside influences in the family.

3. <u>Integration is more difficult for stepfamilies</u>. This may happen because of many reasons including believing you have a traditional family (you don't!) or living the myth that new parents are evil.

Integration may be difficult for many reasons:
- a biological parent with power and influence over family members even if you don't want this person involved
- difficulties in sharing children and with children sharing parents
- feelings of pain and loss surrounding visitation of a parent
- loyalty conflicts for children between biological parents or new parent and biological parent
- competition between "families" and especially between same-sexed adults

- a parent that is suddenly transformed into a magical hero by the children
- new relatives appearing overnight as children try to figure out who sees them next
- the lack of a legal relationship between stepparent and new child.

All of these factors make integration a process of time, hard work, and endurance. While this sounds easy in concept, many stepfamilies do not have the time to wait for things to get better. Frustrations may be very high, and conflict that is inherent in the stepfamily is difficult for people to understand.

In this chapter, we have presented some of the major difficulties stepfamily members face as they try to create a healthy and growth-oriented atmosphere for both adults and children. It is our hope and belief that the forthcoming chapters present helpful information that can be used by stepfamilies seeking positive changes.

Coping With Divorce

It may be unusual to discuss divorce in a book about families, but people in stepfamilies have often experienced divorce and remarriage. And as we will say throughout this book, there are many reasons why stepfamilies are a little bit different from other types of families. Beginning a new family with divorced partners is one of the reasons for this difference.

The word "divorce" has different meanings for all of us. For some it means "failure;" for others it means "relief;" and yet most consider it a mixed blessing. Divorce has become quite commonplace and even somewhat accepted. With millions of adults getting divorced yearly, one wonders if individuals have much choice about its acceptance or at least token acknowledgement. In fact, present statistics show that one out of two marriages end in divorce. Many of these marriages have children and most of these individuals choose to eventually remarry and thus create a stepfamily.

For those of us who have faced divorce, it is probably one of the most difficult and emotional experiences we have ever encountered. Certainly it is one that most individuals do not want to repeat. Sadly enough, many individuals do. As therapists, we think second and third divorces can be avoided. However, it takes some introspection to avoid future hassles.

Joan had been divorced three times and was heading for her fourth. A dominant and persistent individual, her career was always the most important part of her life and her relationships came second. As she reached the top of her profession, she realized that there must be more to life than power and money. Joan had become distant from both her children and her present husband. She felt lonely and sensed that something was missing in her life. Joan hadn't learned what it was like to get close to someone and to give of herself. She was tired of her past patterns and wanted to change.

Looking at your divorce and the person you <u>were</u> in it may influence and help your remarriage. In working with couples, we have seen individuals hamper their present relationships by avoiding dealing with their past. We're not saying that all divorced individuals need to relive their past traumas a la Freudian analysis, but rather that some of the mistaken notions that they have from previous relationships seem to carry right into present ones.

Joe left his first wife because she became too involved in her career and "neglected" their home. During the years that followed, Joe believed he had come to terms with this concept and so he again married a woman who enjoyed her work. After a year of marriage, he was contemplating divorce again. In reality, Joe hadn't come to terms with anything at all. On one hand, he desired a self-sufficient woman who could make decisions and earn a good salary. At the same time, he wanted someone who would take care of him and love doing household chores. He was looking for a miracle worker, a combination of a person that's virtually impossible to find. Joe had seen too many T.V. commercials where the beautiful woman says "I bring home the bacon, cook it, and clean up your mess."

As therapists, we get angry at the way many people look at divorce, particularly when children are involved. It seems like everyone has a stake in your business (friends, relatives, lawyers, I.R.S.). Often you feel like saying, "Get lost." Ending a relationship and admitting that you have failed (and everyone hates to fail) is trauma enough for most of us. Having kids involved in the process just makes things more complicated.

Many times we have seen couples stay in a relationship because of the kids. That's usually a mistake. Miserable people make miserable parents and sometimes they help create miserable kids. So how does this cycle happen?

Well, let's take a look at this for a moment. Parents are strong role models. Statements like "he walks just like his father" or "she talks just like her Mom" are commonplace. Living with someone for many years helps create patterns of behavior, particularly if you are teaching a child the road to adulthood. And that's what parents are supposed to do. The people that kids come to know best and believe in are usually parents. In our work with families, we believe the strongest force in any family is the couple and their marriage. In fact, there's an old saying among family therapists that goes like this: "If a child is disturbed, the marriage is always disturbed." However, if a marriage is disturbed, the kids don't always come out disturbed. Simply put, this means that when we see parents who come to us and say Johnny or Susie is a problem, we know the marriage is always shaky and needs help. So far, we haven't been proven wrong.

Sometimes we see a couple come in and we know they are in bad shape but the kids seem to come out okay. Sometimes a child learns how to cope, but it takes a lot of work and energy for a child to ignore their parents. It's hard enough being a kid without having to figure out that your parents are leading you on the path to unhappiness. It's sad that parents pass down to their children such attributes as child abuse, incest, alcoholism, wife beating, and numerous other afflictions that travel in families for generations. We're not saying that divorce is a cure-all for these families, but sometimes escape is the best measure.

But divorce is worthless if you don't learn anything about yourself during the process. For instance, Sally experienced incest with her father at the age of 11. At 16 years old, she married a man who abused and beat her for five years. After running away in fear, she received a divorce and ended up marrying two more abusers within the span of three years. When Sally became involved in a single parent group, it became obvious her problems weren't just related to being a single parent. She had to learn to get through her past and learn to respect herself for being a human being. She had to see that she was worth something and didn't deserve to be misused. That lesson took Sally years to learn, just like it had taken her years to learn that she was worthless. After more years of pain and torture, Sally finally realized she could be happy if she worked at it. It was not an easy battle, but one where she was the victor and not the victim.

All of us aren't alcoholics, child abusers, or living in severely disturbed families, but still many of us get divorced. A message that is faced by individuals in these circumstances is, "Why not stay together for the children?"

If a couple stays married for their children's sake, they teach their children several messages, including

- that relationships and marriages are unhappy affairs and generally make people sad
- that most couples fight all the time and bicker over silly, inane matters
- that women or men are creeps, insensitive, jealous, etc.
- that children are the major focus in marriage and not the couple's relationship.

Brad and Julie had been married for 10 years and had two children. Their first child was a girl of eight and the boy was five years old. As a couple, the whole neighborhood thought they had a compatible marriage. Like many couples, they hid their problems from everyone, including themselves. As individuals, they seemed agreeable and friendly. Brad was a salesman and traveled quite often. Julie was a school teacher and also attended graduate classes often. Because Brad was often working late, Julie assumed most of the duties in the home and with the children. This was fine--but eventually it had its toll on the relationship. Julie grew resentful and forced Brad to get involved with the kids. They had loud arguments about this issue. This was the beginning of a gradual deterioration.

With kids growing up, Julie became more involved in outside activities and tried to get from friends what she was missing in the marriage. She seemed to have less and less in common with Brad, and their life together grew boring despite their horrendous fights. Towards the end of their relationship, they fought constantly and also verbally abused their children. Like many couples that stay together for the sake of the children, Julie eventually found someone else and the marriage ended.

In light of situations like these, we believe that most people get divorced for good reasons! Even though we know that individuals sometimes are going to deeply hurt spouses, children, and themselves, it is sometimes the best decision for all involved. We believe that most couples work hard to try and make their marriages successful. It is usually after years of struggle that many people think divorce is okay rather than a quick, easy, selfish decision by people who give up easily. In our work with many couples, we have rarely found divorce to be simple. It takes the average person a year to think about pulling out of a relationship. That's just thinking and not actually separating or leaving. Many couples separate three, four, or five times before they make a decision to finally end the grief.

Arnold Lazurus, from Rutgers University, in a recent article discussed a couple who were in constant conflict and desired help. Through work and hard effort, the couple learned how to communicate about all the things that they couldn't previously agree upon. Finally, they stopped fighting and learned how to talk. After all this work, they walked into the counseling office and one of them said, "Dr. Lazurus, you've helped us and done a terrific job. But we wonder if it's worth it. We still have great differences. She likes steak and I like fish, I get up early and she gets up late. In other words, we're just two very different people. We have learned how to compromise but it takes so much work. I think we've realized that maybe it's time for a divorce." This couple learned that there is much to say for marrying someone with similar interests, who believes in things you do. Many couples find this out too late.

Understanding why you got a divorce and the reasons your marriage didn't work can be very helpful for the person considering remarriage, or if you are remarried and experiencing difficulty.

Divorce for the Woman

Like many major crises in life, divorce can leave your life in an uproar. For a woman, divorce can be a brutal reminder that life can be tough. This is especially true when you have children. Over 7 percent of American households are headed by women who are single parents with one or more children at home. The average income for unmarried women with children is often below the poverty level. More than one of every 10 American children is supported by taxpayers. This assistance is usually required not only by family poverty but because of abandonment.

Each of us has heard stories of women who are left alone with children to support and no saleable skills. Ironically, child custody cases sometimes take a unique twist where the mother will lose custody of the children because she cannot support them. However, in most cases, the woman still receives custody of the children with support from the non-custodial parent. Too often, this support is not enough and the woman begins a difficult journey that can lead to a path of dissillusionment and anger.

In addition to financial struggles and trying to develop a career, there are other difficulties for the woman as a single parent. Now she has to do all the things she did before, plus the work her ex-spouse was doing. This means not only financial support in a job, but learning how to do male-oriented jobs like mowing lawns, fixing cars and other objects, and doing all the discipline. This experience can be defeating or frustrating, but sometimes can also lead one to a good sense of security and well-being.

Janie was married for 15 years to a successful doctor. She paid his way through medical school by her job as a nurse and later became his receptionist/nurse/full-time office help. They had three beautiful children and were active in community affairs. One day, Frank came home and said that he had found a younger woman, another doctor working her way up the ladder. Janie was "given" a comfortable settlement by the court but not enough to even pay the taxes on her home. She was bitter and angry at what was left for her after all those years of hard work. But Janie didn't give up. She organized a nursing service with some friends who were in the same circumstances. After several trying years, she started earning a decent living. However, Janie was luckier than many women her age. At least, she had some saleable skills.

If you look at divorce in America, most people do it the wrong way. In our work with divorced clients, most of them had an awful mental and emotional experience. Few people part as friends. The more money one has and the more children one parents, the worse the procedure will be. It's a sad thought that someone with whom you share intimacy and whom you once loved ends up being such a hated foe. We see two main reasons for this. One, people haven't learned how to withdraw, psychologically and emotionally, from people without hurting them. The rule is to protect ourselves from fear by our anger. People believe you can't leave someone whom you still love. The philosophy that you can love your spouse and still not be happily married is not accepted by our culture. However, marriage today takes a lot more than love to make it work.

Secondly, if people haven't already become adversaries in the divorce process, most lawyers will assure that conclusion. They're trained to defend and to win. Their goal is not for you to like your ex-spouse but to get the most you can, even if you destroy the relationship. Money becomes all important. Arguments begin over almost anything and everything. Couples fight over houses, cars, pictures, records, silverware, wedding gifts, ad infinitum. In the end, a person hates not only the ex-spouse but virtually every lawyer in the phonebook. For most of us, that's divorce in America. A joyous experience!

So, it is not unusual that many women who are divorced end up being men-haters. Anything with a penis is a manipulator, controller, and worthy of being loathed. This attitude generally leads to unhappiness and a waste of energy and resources. Generalizations like this lead to aloneness, but sometimes this can be simpler for a person than facing life. If you invest all your energy into hating men, you don't have to face yourself. It keeps you from being dependent and free (something we usually fear); instead, you can be looked at as "the scorned woman."

On the other hand, suppose you get divorced and you still are at least on friendly terms with your spouse. The difficulties still are many. The woman is caught in several dilemmas. Single parent, yet not single parent. Single, but yet somewhat married. The road is not easy.

The concept of a single parent is somewhat misleading. The non-custodial parent often has a lot to say about parenting, wants to be involved in decisions, and even if he's 5,000 miles away, his presence permeates within the family. In many cases, the woman ends up still taking care of the man. Is he okay? Maybe I should help him work out a relationship with the kids? Should I drive the kids to see him? Women are often very good at taking care (of whomever) and so fall into this role rather easily. Sometimes they have all the hassles of being servant without any of the rewards. Dating is a typical example of this. You want to be single and yet you are treated as a rare disease. Mention kids and many males drift away into the moonlight. Mention marriage with kids and they run into the moonlight.

Sally lived with this dilemma. Divorced for three years, her husband still had a key for the house so he could see the kids whenever he wished. Since he was busy on weekends, she often drove the kids 200 miles to see him in order to keep the father-child relationship alive. In therapy, Sally explored some important questions she was neglecting to face. Was it she or the kids who needed this relationship? Could he drive a car as well as she? Did she stay attached to her ex-spouse to keep from facing other men? Was she afraid of what her kids would say if she started dating?

Feeling sorry for yourself and wanting to marry anything that walks and talks to you can also be a consideration at this time. Relationships can get to be a hassle. You get tired of running a house, kids, and working, but yet there's <u>some</u> independence, maybe the most you've ever had. A male can be a threat to that independence. Often you want roles to change if you were to date someone or eventually marry. You want someone to accept your kids and you. That process is difficult and a much different commitment than one you may have made when you were 18 years old. You don't want to fail next time and you want things done your way. You want more equality. The funny thing is you haven't had much practice at this new you, but it sounds and feels good.

Divorce for the Man

The male, too, feels like he's a failure. Dealing with both love for an ex-spouse and yet anger and hatred at the same time. The disappointment! Why did I ever get involved? I tried hard. Wanting to blame the other partner for all that happened but inwardly knowing that he also had a part, and not knowing how to change and make it better. Afraid of being alone with no one to disagree. Realizing that he has to start all over again, maybe losing the kids! The recognition that the relationship will change and never be quite the same. Wanting to be a part of his kids' lives and realizing that it's very hard.

After 20 years of marriage, Gary felt all of these things. With two older sons and a daughter in high school, he decided to leave. His relationship with Joanne seemed unfulfilling, like much of his life. He had reached a good management position, but there <u>must</u> be more to life. He tried to explain his feelings to Joanne but she couldn't understand.

Maybe I'll quit and start my own business. Maybe I'll just travel or hide somewhere. When he told Joanne that it was over she told him she would get from him "all that she could." "I'll be left alone without a job. I've lived my whole life for you," she said. Gary's life had become so complicated. It had all seemed so easy a few years ago. "Even the kids were on Joanne's side," he muttered. Starting a new life was not going to be easy for Gary.

So, where do you go from here? Maybe you have found someone else or need someone to talk to about what is happening to you. Many men want to withdraw from life or else pretend that they're 20 years old and single. Sometimes they try to experience 10 years in one. Usually, relationships appear superficial at first. It's difficult being happy with someone when you're used to sharing in depth with a spouse. Men like to be taken care of and now no one gives a damn. And worse, a question keeps haunting you, "How do I reach the kids?" You're experiencing new things, trying to be freer and changing but they want the same old Dad. Yet, you couldn't be even if you want to be.

At first, Larry wanted to be everything for his kids. "But then I got tired of being super-Dad. All the presents and the movies. I got out of my relationship because I wanted to be real. I figured if my kids didn't like me for what I was or <u>rather</u> what I was becoming, the hell with it."

Traditionally, males are taught to be providers and supporters. In the career world, they're looked at as decision makers. Now they're keeping house, eating out, making their own meals, and having to leave the house they worked so hard to buy. All the things a man may have wanted are taken away and there's nothing to fill the gap. Just being yourself isn't enough.

Jack used to have nightmares and think he was going crazy. "I still dream about wanting to kill her. I'm so angry about her finding someone else and kicking me out of my own house. She acts as if I'm some terrible disease. I still can't understand what happened. I know that we were having problems but she never shared with me about how she was feeling. I just feel like my whole world is a whirlwind, I can't seem to make sense of this."

So, how do these two new types of people unite, as is the case in the stepfamily? Single women with children are looking for a new relationship with equality, maybe a sensitive male who is accepting of her new career and willing to love her children as much as he loves her. And the male is possibly confused about his role, wanting to be taken care of and yet supporting the new career woman. How will they ever make a go of it?

The expectations, desires, past messages, failures, needs for security, families, relatives! Where does it all begin and end? Relationships used to be easy but now it's never going to be the same. Once divorced, always cautious. All the people who seemed to be a part of your life, such as boyfriends, girlfriends, ex-spouses, children, parents, and friends, are different. You want to be sure this time but you know the odds are even higher. You're not worried about forming a relationship, but rather you're trying to keep this circus from driving you insane. Finding someone and falling in love may be more of a hassle than you ever anticipated. Coping with the divorce won't end now. Many things will come up after you've remarried and are trying the second time around, but at least you've got somewhat of a perspective of what's happening to you. Getting your life together after a divorce is a tremendous task. Some folks never quite make it and would rather live in their past. Others decide that life is worth it and get on with it.

Beginning New Relationships

Love is an exciting word. It conjures up all sorts of images for many of us. Love means different things for a 16-year-old than for someone who is a mature adult. Some of what is called love is actually infatuation, but it's difficult to separate the terms. We're going to look at this process of love, particularly for the divorced person with children and the potential stepfamily member.

After getting a divorce, most people don't know how they feel about themselves or the opposite sex. Usually they have been rejected by an ex-spouse in numerous ways and it is easy to develop hangups about looks, sexuality, conversation skills, and numerous other attributes. Many of us like to retreat by working all hours of the day or night.

Greg felt this was the easiest way to cope. "I had worked my way to the top by practically living my job. Besides all the nights I brought work home and all the places I traveled, it was usually the weekend that upset Sherry the most. If we had a free night, I'd always entertain clients or stay home and sleep. She got tired of the whole grind and felt really bored. I tried to change but I was afraid I'd lose my job or be stuck where I was. So finally she left and I was really at a loss. I didn't know what to do. Maybe I should have taken some time for myself but the pain was too much. Instead I kept spending time at the job, even more than before. Going home was lonely and I tried to be there as little as possible. But you know, even in all my work I felt a piece of me was missing. I still was so damn lonely. Finally I figured out that the problem was me and that it wouldn't be solved unless I took a good look at myself and my life."

One may think of the opposite sex as worthless and so they are "worth" avoiding. Others get invested in their children's lives and spend all hours at their activities. Eventually much of this avoidance wears thin. The problem is that once we've had a deep relationship and experienced love (no matter how short it was) it's tough to forget and live without it. As human beings, life is more exciting and worthwhile when shared with someone else who understands us. So, generally, we lick our wounds and recover. Some in six months and some in six years. But we go on searching for that someone. This time it will be different. This time he or she will be just right. This person will look great, talk intelligently, and listen to our every whim.

Initially, that's usually how it goes. It's after marriage that life begins to change. The "institution" seems to have a knack for bringing us to our senses. We've discovered that many couples think this infatuation stage should last forever. That's an impossible task. As Roy Schneider stated one time in an interview, "If I stayed like I am when I first fell in love, I'd never get a damn thing done in life."

Falling in love is a great experience but that feeling doesn't last forever. It changes into deeper emotions with time and the right person.

So suppose you're looking for someone to love. How does this process go for most of us? Difficult at best! Searching for that perfect someone at the job or cocktail parties, social organizations, or even at the singles bar is hazardous. Most people get angry and frustrated. Single life isn't all it's supposed to be for the divorced person. After all, there's a major difference between you and other "single" peers. You've been in love before. Having progressed for years into a state of an intimate relationship, you know what it is like. And, like most human beings, you remember both the good and the bad.

It's interesting that after you divorce someone, that person may seem more attractive to you even if you are extremely angry with him or her. Some of that comes from the closeness of finally being able to communicate. It may be over the children, the furniture, or telling them that it is finally over, but you learn to share. It's often sad that it comes just too late. When the engine finally breaks down in your car, you know you have to get another car. A major overhaul won't do. You've got to say goodbye.

Ann found that parting was the most difficult thing she had ever done. "Saying goodbye to Dennis just tore me up. It took me years to get up the courage to tell him it was over. The funny thing was that it really didn't take either of us by surprise. We both knew that our relationship hadn't been good for either one of us. But asking someone to walk out the door and the person actually doing it are two different things. I felt like the biggest creep in the world. I still love him but I just can't live with him. We each do too much damage."

Let's face it, most of us have fond memories of that old car, the one you had to kick and scream at on the side of the road. The same is true of past relationships. The pain and hurt hopefully diminishes. You remember the good times and the attempts you made to work it out. When we think of the other person, some of us are filled with vengeance but most just feel tinges of regret. What did I do wrong? Couldn't we have made it? Songwriters know our hearts and many write lyrics that portray these images. It's sad for relationships to change, and a lot of anger comes from this sadness, but eventually it withers away.

In therapy, John didn't know what to do with all his anger. "It seems like I'm mad at everybody; my boss, my secretary, and my kids. The funny thing is, I can't be mad at her. When I talk to her I just feel this emptiness in my stomach. It's overwhelming. Life without her means nothing to me. How could she just end our marriage? I just don't understand what happened."

You may get mad at your ex-spouse because she has the children or angry at him because he's not there to help or he's acting like a Santa Claus, but mostly it's loneliness. After touching and being touched, it's difficult to live without intimacy. If there's ever a resounding melody behind a marriage, it's loneliness. It sometimes gets in our way of making clear decisions. We forget our part in the first relationship and how things must change if things are to get better the second time. Sometimes each of us tends to view past relationships with so much nostalgia, that we end up remarrying someone just like our first mate.

This usually leads to trouble and failure. If we grab someone to help with the battle, then the road will be bumpy indeed! Finding someone to fill our loneliness is easy. Finding someone to love is more difficult.

Susan fell into this trap rather easily. "I felt so lonely that I dated Bob out of my need for someone or something. It sounds crazy but I wanted my independence and yet I couldn't stand to be alone. When I married Bob, I found I was reliving my first marriage in a matter of months. I was reliving all the same hassles and problems. It was like a recurring nightmare."

To make things even harder, you may not be the same person that married someone else 5, 10, or 20 years ago. Like Susan, you've been changing and maybe haven't taken a look at the new you along the way. After a divorce, people need to re-evaluate priorities. Is work important? How will I feel sexually? Will I travel more? Will I buy things I always wanted to? Will I try to be less serious? Will I be free or sane controlled? The list goes on and on. Divorce can be a very introspective process. A chance to look at you and what you may have been avoiding about yourself for many years.

After Divorce for the Woman

The area of sexuality can be a difficult one in both males or females and certainly one for introspection. For the female, it can be an uphill struggle. Many divorces involve inadequate sexual practices. Usually both partners are the cause but one gets the blame. For several reasons, it often ends up being the woman and she may even venture to see a sex therapist. She believes she is frigid, non-orgasmic, or just doesn't know how to "turn on" a man. All these symptoms may just be a reflection of an inadequate relationship or one where the love had vanished.

Cindy thought she was a sexual misfit until she got divorced. "I thought sex was something that you had to do. All those wondrous magazines talked about orgasm as if it was like eating ice cream. Everybody does it. Well, I guess I wasn't everybody. Fred just got his kicks and it was over in a few minutes. When I asked him to get some therapy with me he said it was my problem. In a way, he was right. My problem was him. After I got divorced, Tim showed me that I wasn't crazy. That sex could be both caring and fun. It was like opening a whole new world for me. I may not have 50 orgasms a day, but I feel close to someone when I go to bed."

Sometimes, too, the woman may use sex as a weapon within the relationship. Sort of a "if you're nice you'll get some" ultimatum. After a while, you sometimes lose track of the game from reality and don't know how to love but rather only how to play the game. This ends up frightening and frustrating for all involved.

Besides these games, it is true that the sexual activity of many divorced persons is rather dismal in the later stages of a marriage. It is not uncommon for therapists to hear couples say that they haven't experienced intercourse on a regular basis for several years. In marriage counseling, we rarely see a troubled marriage that has a vibrant sexual relationship. No matter what you read in the newspapers, sex usually involves love and commitment. In all honesty, these ingredients help make "good sex." In our opinion, sex seems inadequate without caring. So when you've had problems (which most divorced couples have had for years), it would be logical that your sex life does.

Usually the couple comes into therapy blaming each other. Diane thought Jon was too macho. "He just is in it for himself. Whenever he wants sex, I'm supposed to cry for joy. Well, it just doesn't seem fun for me." On the other hand, Fred feels neglected. "It's like I have to beg for sex. If I behave a certain way and I do what she wants, I get rewarded. I feel like I'm a dog who begs for a bone."

So when a marriage ends and you are a single female or male, you probably have all sorts of doubts. Sometimes they are for good reasons. You've been basically on the reserve shelf for a while and you may wonder if you know how to relate to anyone. Secondly, you may be confused. By all accounts you read, you should be madly making love on your front lawn with all the other single folks. Somehow you feel vaguely uncomfortable with this assumption. Life at the condominium may not be for you.

"I feel out of place here," states Jack, a 42-year-old business executive. "I never was very good with giggling girls. I'm looking for someone who's mature. I'm not looking for a sexual relationship. I'm looking for a <u>relationship</u>. I need someone to care for me."

Some of these self-doubts come from other reasons. You may have had an inadequate partner and thus you don't even know what a "good" sexual relationship is. Most of us haven't had that many encounters. It's not like driving a car. If you had sex with 10 people before you married, that may be many times more than for many women or men. You may think you're deformed in some fashion. You might have received messages for years that you are lousy in bed. So suddenly here's your chance. What do you do? Grab someone on the corner, "Hey buddy, I think I'm inadequate (or at least that's what I've been told). Could we check this out?" Probably this is not for you.

This approach seems a bit asinine but it's not too far from the truth. Most people want to find out their sexual needs but requirements for a partner are absurd. You want someone who really cares but doesn't want to get attached.

Take the case of Suzanne, for an example. She was married for 10 years to a singer of a local band and was tired of the whole routine. As a school teacher, she was excellent. As a lover, she was wondering what happened. At first, their sexual relationship was great but it's been downhill since. The last year it has been virtually nonexistent. Joe says, "she's an awful lover and frigid." She says, "he's in a hurry and exceedingly horny." Suzanne also suspects that he is seeing someone else. One day Joe says he's going to spend more time on the road because they need the money. She says, you take the job and I'm leaving. He takes the job and she files for divorce.

Suzanne sees a therapist after the divorce and tries to make sense of it all. At first she tries to avoid the topic of sexuality but eventually reveals her doubts in humorous undertones. After being in therapy for several months, she meets a caring man who invites her for a weekend rendezvous. To test her lover on the first night she rejects his advances. With quiet understanding her friend agrees. On the second night, Suzanne agrees and experiences a sexual relationship that is satisfying and ego strengthening. She begins to realize that poor relationships make for poor sex and that caring sex is a process that involves two people and not just one. Suzanne had been blaming herself all these years for a problem that involved two people and not just her. Sometimes inadequate sex is simply poor chemistry between a couple.

Others may play the sexual game in a different fashion. Some women may hide behind insecurities by playing games and acting as if they were the virtuous virgin who has never experienced sex or slept with a man. Jackie would be an example of this breed. Invited for a weekend by an older and established businessman, she pretends that she does not know what will occur. She brings two sets of clothes (sexy and virginal) and does not dare to discuss the nature of the weekend. Most assuredly she will torment the male to all extremes possibly and eventually may submit her newfound virginity in a lost moment of ignorance while under the influence of alcohol. She will feign all knowledge of the incident in the morning and regret having ever done such a dastardly deed. Jackie's games help her ignore the realities of being an older woman and divorced. She resorts to patterns of younger years, but the males' tolerance is more limited than when he or she was 18 years old.

After Divorce for the Male

For the male, women like Jackie are just a part of his dilemma. The male's journey of relative insecurity after a divorce is threatening and scary. No longer the youth he was, the male is often competing against a younger, fitter image of himself. He, too, questions his sexuality. Probably, for years, he has been wondering if he is sexually okay and desirable to another woman. Most males set their sights on a partner whom they perceive as less or equal to them and rarely do they set goals for the "unattainable." This would be too threatening and so he picks a person with whom he can be superior.

Ted fell into this trap. "I have a strong need to be boss and so I keep on picking these dependent type of women. A woman who is strong is scary to me and not worth the hassle. When I pick someone dependent, she usually gets too clingy and I want to leave. On the other hand, an independent woman resents my bossiness and ends up telling me to get lost. I've been working on changing my perspective but it gets hard."

So the male debates about his "perfect" partner, the slim, trim, vivacious women that he has always longed for and desired. Too often, this image is unrealistic and soon sorry males realize that it is nice to have someone to talk to about life's difficulties. Loneliness can be a harrowing experience for the male. Used to having everything done for him, suddenly he must shop, clean, launder his clothes, and make his own meals (or eat out). Most males find this experience difficult and look for someone to take care of them. Of any group, males who had the most rigid and conservative sex role patterns in their marriage have the most difficulty coping with divorce.

Males also deal with the concept of failure in a marriage differently than women do. Much energy is usually focused on career goals, but again most successful career men have a woman who is supportive. The myth of "behind every successful man there is a woman" is not all myth. Usually work can only satisfy the male if he has a settled home life. Substituting work for a lover wears thin on the emotional psyche. If the male doesn't have a support system at home, even work can become uninteresting.

The male may also be the most reluctant person in establishing a new relationship. It is typical for the male to take a financial beating in a divorce case and sometimes he cannot afford to get remarried. Also, the scars of losing a relationship can be deep, especially since many males project feelings inward and have difficulty releasing their guilt and hostility. This leads to the feeling that all women are "bad" and continues the fear of rejection. This may be the person who becomes "macho" and uses women for whatever he can get. Rather than face his feelings inside, the macho male puts up an impenetrable wall and sees relationships as endless sexual encounters. Trapped in his bitterness, he begins to run out of prospects as his partners realize his endless selfish needs.

A Final Mate

If males and females can overcome their doubts and try again, romance can be fulfilling. Relationships the second time around usually progress to a deeper level and at a faster rate. This is because you may seek more intimacy and are tired of playing games with other people. The relationships may have a maturer note, particularly if children are involved. Children are a part of the relationship and courting but, hopefully, <u>not</u> the major part. The initial focus of any relationship should be on the couple and how they can get enjoyment and happy memories from this experience. That is why the beginning of a relationship is so exciting. It's like walking on air. You feel happy, silly, confused, and madly in love with someone. You sneak around to spend special moments with them. Your lover is constantly on your mind. Life is a whirlpool of thoughts and it's difficult to keep focus on anything else. Even money doesn't seem to matter! When we look at relationships, we call this the ecstacy or the first stage of intimacy. It can last from one month to six months or a year. Sometimes you may want it to last forever.

The second or "realistic" stage begins a period of change for the couple. They begin to feel somewhat serious about the relationship and start contemplating its future. Romance is still alive and well, but money is considered and discussed: Who pays? Can we afford to do that? This is the period where the couple is testing each other out and seeing if each person is going to hang in the relationship. This period is usually shorter and is almost an interim process between first and third stages.

The last or commitment stage is where a couple finally decides that the relationship is very serious and worthy of consideration for marriage. With the stepfamily, some serious topics and agendas are discussed then, as is often the case with a "first time" married couple. Usually each person, or at least one, has been in a relationship before and they have an idea of what can go wrong. The only problem is that with a stepfamily they usually discuss surface matters but are afraid to deal with real issues. After all, the future spouse may run away if the marriage appears too hard. Children will be involved and this will bring both considerable happiness and problems for the remarried couple. Many times each person will attempt to relive past marriages and discuss how things "were" or how things "weren't" with an ex-spouse. This has some value but after a while it creates resentment and jealousy. The newly remarried couple needs to set their own course and to forget the past as much as possible. They will have enough haunting memories and we see little need to create more. Getting a good start when you get married isn't just luck or good mating practice; it takes good communication and a willingness to face reality.

Money From Divorce

Why do people want to get married when they've probably already failed once in the process and have a few children to add to the fire? When you look at the divorce rate in America we generally have a 50-50 chance of making it. Those odds are not so favorable.

For most divorced men or women living as a single person is a temporary phase. Most divorced persons remarry within three years after a divorce. Current figures estimate about 75 percent of women and even a higher portion of men remarry.

The truth is that marriage has considerable value within our culture and society. It is a strong form of commitment and bonding. Most people view marriage as a permanent proposition. In other words, we don't go into marriage expecting it to fail and not to work. Many divorced parents remarry because they need assistance. Remarriage improves a financial situation, ends loneliness and isolation, enables contact with new friends or couples, makes one "normal" to peers, and provides a parent to children. Remarriage in our culture has not changed since the days of our first ancestors. In the old colonies, people remarried after a spouse died because they needed other folks in order to survive the harsh environment. Basically, the same is true for most of us today.

With the stepfamily, the commitment should even be stronger than the first or traditional marriage. Many people are not only trying marriage for the second time but are also involving children from a first marriage. This is a high-risk game. Everyone might be betting that you won't make it ... kids, parents, ex-spouses. You certainly can't conclude that they'll be on your side. The problem is that most couples don't know how to begin preparing for remarriage and the stepfamily. So when difficulties come up, they appear out of proportion compared to the type or manner of problem we're used to seeing in the traditional ma, pa, and two kids family. The stepfamily is sort of like combat. When you're ready for the battles, you can fight effectively and win your battle for freedom (democracy and the American way!). But those sneak attacks when you're not ready will get you every time. So, many folks are unprepared for stepfamily uproar and want to quit. "I'VE HAD ENOUGH OF THIS STUFF! YOU CAN HAVE THIS FAMILY!!" You get defeated, you don't know what to do, and so you leave. There are plenty of reasons for supporting your actions. After all, there are no models for help in most circumstances. What you learned from your first marriage or from Mom and Dad just doesn't work for the stepfamily. So you're stuck in a system with no rules to play to win. Well, that's one of the reasons we wrote this book! Another is that we had to go through all this misery in our own family and we're trying to let you get by a little easier. But remember, a little misery won't hurt that much.

And, there will be joy. Believe us, it will come! But it helps to hang in there. Most folks say it takes two years for a remarriage to get on the right track. We believe that's true. Two years of misery and joy in mixed packages. But undertaking the pitfalls can be very helpful.

One of the most important ways we have found helpful to get on the right track is to look at some of the problems that might occur in your marriage <u>before</u> you get married rather than after the fact. Some of these potential concerns reflect directly upon the stepfamily and its peculiar mix of people and situations.

When we work with remarried couples, we see four areas that are potential sticks of dynamite: money, family roles, children, and sex. Let's take a look at these in some detail.

I. <u>Money</u>:

This area means freedom for many individuals. Freedom to do the things you want to do, choice of lifestyle that you desire, and an opportunity to buy the necessities and luxuries of life. It can also become a virtual battleground for a couple.

For example, Sallie, a single parent, has decided to get remarried. However, she has serious reservations which she has failed to discuss. She has been the head of her household and although she would like more money, she is not going to pay homage to any male for his income. She is not so sure about including her savings into the dual fund of the couple since she has saved more than he. Sallie would also like to have her own checking account and believes she is more competent at writing and handling the bills than her future mate.

She is also cautious about both money and saving it since her first husband left her with nothing. This time she will make sure she has a little nest egg in case of failure.

Harry, on the other hand, is a little different. Stung for a loss of $150,000 in his first marriage, he is going to do it right this time. Under no circumstances will he ever let his wife know what he makes for a living. He will provide nice comforts for everyone and sign all of the bills. Harry will have his separate accounts and also joint accounts with his new wife. However, she will be expected to be totally up front with him and share all her resources.

In our opinion, both Sallie and Harry are heading for trouble. Money is an important part of the modern relationship, but when it is the major focal point you are in trouble. We believe negotiation is the key to keeping money in its proper place within the marriage. For a second marriage, money becomes more of a factor because you have had your struggles and you're tired of them. You've worked hard for some security that you don't want to see thrown away. First marrieds usually struggle together and learn how to see their financial picture as a twosome. Remarrieds in the stepfamily have more ideas regarding finances and don't take many things for granted. Here are some items that need to be discussed before (rather than after) the marriage.

1. Past financial assets and problems with previous mate. Who did what and why? If your wife or husband was a big spender, don't force other people to live by that image.

2. An honest discussion of present assets and what you will bring into the relationship. After all, it _is_ a partnership. Don't play games with each other. If need be, outline in a legal contract what is hers and what is his if the relationship should end. Protect yourself if you are worried. Most lawyers will be glad to help you set up a legal agreement.

3. Even if you are worried, don't place money in between the two of you. Mutually discuss your financial relationship and resources. Talk about how you think money should be spent and saved. What is the financial responsibility of each partner? Come to an agreement of what the responsibilities are for each of you in the marriage. If not, you will fight this battle forever.

4. Look at the financial sex roles. Does she work? Is he the breadwinner? More likely, both will work. What does that mean to the relationship? Joint or separate accounts? Who decides spending on what items? Who pays the bills? The role of the "good provider" or the male breadwinner is soon disappearing in American society. Sex roles are being shared more equally, but stubbornly, by both sexes.

Two-wage and dual-career households are having a major effect on the family and most people are having difficulty coping with sex-role problems.

5. Determine your material possessions before you buy or rent a living space. Who will bring what types of furniture? Do you discard items which remind you of an ex-spouse? Should you sell everything and start all over? For instance, Lou had trouble sitting in his own living room because of his dislike for the furniture. Half of it reminded him of his past life with his ex-wife and the other half contained memories between the kids and his new wife, Mary. All in all, sitting at home got to be an unpleasant experience. For his peace of mind and for the family's sanity, Lou and Mary decided to spend the extra money for new furniture rather than to live in the past.

6. Discuss spending money on the kids. How much do they cost? Would you want more children? Even if you get child support, it's usually not nearly enough. Discuss the new parent's role in supporting children. And no matter what people tell you, children cost money. If child support is minimal, one should be certain that the new spouse is willing to contribute to the family or else there will be big trouble. Placing money or children in the

middle of a marriage will split it apart. If you put both money and children, start packing your bags.

II. <u>Family Roles</u>:

If there was one area which has changed dramatically in the last decade, it is sex roles within the family. Both men and women are more confused than ever. In a nutshell, the biggest equal rights fight is within the home. With both parents working, most women are tired of doing a full-time job plus cleaning house, doing laundry, raising kids, and cooking meals. Most men are starting to give some help (usually reluctantly) and will be expected to give even more in the future. Some of the areas that need to be discussed in detail (and maybe even in a written contract) are meal cooking, household chores, shopping, household shopping, daily errand running, yard cleaning, car repairs and cleaning, clothes washing, ironing, dishwashing, and home repairs. The list could be endless but if you can get some resolution as to who does what, where, and when, your problems should be somewhat diminished. Our motto with couples is "the less you talk, the more angry you'll get."

However, it's also good to not get overinvolved with dividing chores. Sharon and Phil had everything split up and divided so that even their sweat was divided appropriately. They seemed to be constantly checking lists to see who was to do what. Eventually they put all the chores and duties on their home computer. They felt so regimented in their marriage that they thought they were in the army.

Equality is certainly an appropriate goal but one that is difficult to reach. In our opinion, the best marriages have partners that help each other frequently without worrying about their sex roles. They transcend equality into mutuality without watching their John Wayne or Gloria Steinem parts get in the way.

III. <u>Children</u>:

As people blissfully saunter into marriage, they may forget to talk about any of the kids and be surprised by the tornado that is rampaging a couple's family file. Besides money factors, there are many questions that need to be answered when considering the children. For instance, how is child discipline to be handled? His, her's, or ours? We'll talk more about this specific dilemma in a later chapter. Other issues include: What do you call the step-parent? What name do the children use? Should they be involved in helping plan or participate in the wedding? How do each of you get "space" or "time" away from the kids?

When working with parents, we set some hard and fast rules if a family really wants to make a go of it. We also assume the parents are "in charge" and will provide adequate role models. For example, we insist that the stepparent be called Mom or Dad. They do what Moms and Dads "do" and likewise deserve the honor of the title. We feel it's important for kids to get in the proper frame of mind from the beginning and calling someone Joe or Suzie just doesn't help. We require this _even_ if the stepparent doesn't like it. Maybe if they have the title, they'll act the part. We've seen it happen. Some of our colleagues and members of step-families disagree with this concept. However, we believe that in most cases it is helpful. Often the new stepfamily doesn't want to commit to being a family and thus resists being healthy. They let "roles" get in the way of their love. Unwittingly, some therapists contribute to this dilemma. Because they only believe in the traditional family, or due to their own past divorce traumas, this type of therapist insists that the family stay in traditional roles. Phrases like "remember there's only one Mom or Dad" permeate the counseling session. This type of therapist hinders rather than helps a stepfamily.

When we work with families, our way of thinking is quite contrary to the old philosophy. If you are acting as a Mom or Dad do (even on a part-time basis), then you deserve this title. The only time we don't insist on this title is when a child sees a stepparent for only rare visits or infrequently.

We believe actions speak louder than words and that parents set the guidelines for appropriate actions and take the lead in the family. For instance, last names are often a major hassle and a legal triangle. It's too bad our legal system is so crazy that kids have mismatched names with their parents and are immediately identified as different. "Hi, I'm

Sam Jones and this is my son, Joe. No, Joe Smith, not Joe Jones. He's sort of mine but not really. Well, I just pay the bills." We will talk about this in a later chapter because it becomes more of a problem as relationships develop. However, we give one rule of thumb for remarrieds. If everyone can have the same name, do it. If your school is willing to give a little and call your child by his or her new family name without being able to legally change it, push for it. It will psychologically be a lot healthier for the custodial parent and the child than having a child with a distorted or confused identity. In addition, identity is helped by each child having a space or room within the new home or apartment. This space should be planned beforehand and discussed as if everyone's moving into a new house, even if all family members are not new.

We also believe that kids should be involved in the wedding ceremony whether they like it or not. By this, we especially mean kids that will be living with you. If only out of respect and love for the custodial parent, the wedding symbolizes the birth of a new family and so that means everyone is involved. Pouting and crying children are not allowed and are certainly discouraged by proper discipline and discussion. Angry adolescents can learn that loving a parent means trying to open their hearts and minds to others. Too often we have seen that parents, not the child, are the major blocks for a child's resistance.

IV. <u>Sex</u>:

This usually goes okay until one gets married and then it goes away with the romance. One of the things we emphasize with couples is their being open and honest about what they expect their sexual life to be like after they settle in together. Taking time out for romance is very important. Avoiding the pitfalls of the first marriage may be even more vital. Remarrieds often set up the spouse as wonder-plus who will be the perfect sex-mate. The person who will do the rights that the first spouse did wrong. Then they find out the same things go wrong in the second marriage. A long discussion about sex and expectations before marriage may help eliminate problem areas. If you are having sexual problems before marriage, you will most likely have the same problems after you take your vows. In this instance, see a marriage counselor who is knowledgeable in sex therapy. Remember, too, keep the kids out of your bedroom and your sex life. Poor sex is often a symptom that something is going astray in the relationship. At times like these, you need to face up to problems. Talk and discuss what is happening to your relationship, not what is going on in the bedroom. If you're avoiding each other, or don't enjoy spending time with each other, then a discussion is in order. Sometimes we like to hide from things because we hope they'll go away. Relationship problems and sexual difficulties just don't go away. They need to be discussed and cleared up. If you can talk about your personal areas and share what is on your mind (no matter how hard it is), then you are off to a good start. Dealing with problems when they are small and happening "right now" is much better than storing the anger you feel so you can use it at another time. In counseling couples, we have found that sex is almost an unspoken or forbidden topic. It is hard to discuss and problems are usually brushed away. Eventually these problems become major barriers in a couple's relationship.

Parents or In-Laws

Parental involvement may also be a concern for those beginning a stepfamily. It is often true that the first wedding is for one's parents and not really for the couple. Many times parents of a remarried couple will not be approving of a new marriage for several reasons:

<u>Overprotection</u>: No matter how good he or she is, you'll get divorced again.

<u>Identity with ex-spouse</u>: Oh, how horrible that the kids will have a new Mom or Dad.

<u>Remarriage</u>: It's bad enough you get divorced, but <u>never</u> remarriage. Parents may not believe in either.

<u>Fear of change</u>: Parents like things to stay as they are, particularly if you are dependent on them (that's how parents get to feel good). Don't get independent or we'll threaten you with the loss of our love.

No relationship: Your parents may not have a relationship with the spouse in remarriage. There is usually no asking for the daughter's hand. Parents of the spouse do not need to meet the other spouse's parents. There is no investment for them in the remarriage compared to a first marriage.

Often parents will take a wait-and-see attitude with a remarriage and stepfamily. This can make you angry because parental acceptance is one of the keys in life to feeling good. But, even if this is true, life goes on without Mom and Dad. You have your life and happiness to consider and if your parents are disapproving of your remarriage, then that is their choice. Some parents will even force you to choose between them and a new spouse because of the way that they treat him or her or act toward this person. Well, you can't go to sleep with Mom or Dad and you can't grow old with them, either. Forcing you to make a choice like that only makes the relationship between parents and children that much harder. As you get older, parents need to be more like friends and less like parents. Too bad it takes a lifetime for some folks to figure that out.

Sometimes a couple's parents aren't invited to a remarriage ceremony because of the hassles involved. However, because of the lack of parents and children, it may lack a sense of legitimacy. Many couples end up going to a courthouse or a minister because they believe that this time the ceremony is for them and doesn't need all the pomp and circumstance.

Even if this assumption is correct, we still advise couples to consider getting the children involved in the ceremony. It affords the remarriage a sense of authenticity that may be missing otherwise. Get them to be a part. Make up a wedding where they admit the new parent into the family. Have the parent accept the children as part of the ceremony. Each person can then realize that this is for real and not a game. You *will* be living together so let's try to make it work.

A final issue to consider when looking at the remarriage is the idea of the honeymoon. Often stepfamily couples don't take a honeymoon (for many valid reasons) and usually step right into the home and family. We think this may not be the wisest decision. Take a honeymoon if you can. It shows the kids and everyone else that you're in love and you mean it. If you can't afford it, send the kids away and honeymoon at home for a few days. Probably having the house to yourselves for a week or two is good with a remarriage. It gives the new parent a chance to get used to the surroundings and the "parents" may do some redecorating if they wish, to make the home more like "ours" rather than his or hers. If you're moving into a new residence, take some time off before moving. This may make it easier for you when the kids come back and they realize the new parent has an important say in what goes on in the house. You're not an outsider anymore; rather, it's important that both the parents demonstrate that they belong and will be contributors whether members agree with this or do not agree. Remember, kids don't pay the rent, you both do.

The Role of Children When
Deciding to Remarry

We've discussed in Chapter II that falling in love is one of the most exciting things that happens to most of us. It's a time of high energy, a time when our world and each day seems very worthwhile. Personally, that feeling would be nice all the time. But that just doesn't happen. "Infatuation" changes to a different state, hopefully one of deeper love without those "blinders" on. Sometimes, though, "blinders" make life a lot easier. When you first meet someone, you like everything about the person and brush over those faults that soon may drive you crazy. However, your faults are parts of you just like your good points. It's too bad that often couples focus on the negative between or about each other rather than the positive. Most of us try to hide our faults because there is a risk of getting hurt or revealing something that one is not proud of or willing to share. As counselors, we help couples and families see that faults are matters that should be handled gently and not in a fit of anger.

We also believe love is full of change and compromise. That's something that will be discussed numerous times in this book. These concepts of change become even more important when you throw a few children into the tangle of romance. Sometimes this can be an awfully frustrating experience and the ramifications carry right into the eventual family unit. When this happens, you're fighting a losing battle right from the start. And that's something none of us wants to get into. Let's look at some ways of making this beginning a successful point, or at least one of less animosity.

When things get complicated, it often feels like you get steamrolled into doing things you're not quite sure you want to do. Sometimes sorting things out can help put life in a proper perspective and help establish your priorities. And what most people want is a real family--not everyone running off and doing whatever they please. We believe people want a sense of unity, a sense of belonging. Family is something that makes life more fulfilling and worthwhile. It's a place where you can be yourself and be accepted for all your strange quirks and ways. Hopefully, it's also a place where you'll be appreciated and recognized for all the things you do for other members of the family.

In our work with couples and families, we find lots of people in families have trouble reaching these goals, not just those in the stepfamily. It's just that being in a stepfamily is sometimes a little more difficult. But we have faith that you have the stamina and the drive to make it work. Love can be a powerful force. And in our perspective, nothing can be more worth fighting for than a strong family.

Even with all that hard work and love you put in, there is still something else to consider. The stepfamily is a different family form than our culture is used to. People are still trying to accept divorce and there are still certain stigmas attached to divorced people. Millions of couples experience great pain in getting a divorce. Years later they're still in mourning. We believe pain is and always will be a part of this experience. However, we also think that society and our culture make life even more difficult for the divorced. Let's face it, there are still many people who don't accept divorce. Along with that, there are even more people who don't understand a stepfamily. They give lip service but there are parents, family, friends, workmates, doctors, lawyers, psychologists, etc., who don't really accept or understand what you're going through. Sometimes just little subtle remarks can make you angry. However, it would be impossible and a waste of energy to try and change everyone's opinion. We believe it is more important to devote your time to making your life better rather than trying to influence what other people think of you. It's a lot more worthwhile to work on your own family, that's more than enough to keep you busy. So let's start thinking.

When you think about how all this started or is starting, the kids are not usually the top priority when you are falling in love. You may try to convince yourself that they are, but their hearts aren't beating 90 miles an hour, they aren't running around cleaning house like a mad person because he or she is coming over. Most kids don't have the concept of love that adults have. They aren't grown up and their concepts are young and not developed. Adults know that love can be an enriching process, but it involves a lot more than fairytale romance.

That's why adults play so many games with each other. Most of the time, they're scared. Scared the other won't like parts of them, or afraid to make the commitment to lasting relationships.

Add some kids to these notions and you know that it takes commitment for a couple in a stepfamily. It's not like you're 17 and if it doesn't work out you can leave. Whenever kids are involved (even when they hate you), leaving can be very difficult. With all the hassle you still will work harder in the stepfamily than you ever have before. We're not going to lie to you and tell you things will be easy. Most people in stepfamilies have at least one member (and usually two) who have been divorced and they know that leaving a family is easier said than done. You want things to work and straightening out expectations with the kids is important from the beginning.

Sometimes, kids can be quite a hassle when you are getting love started. After all, you're not marrying them, although it seems like you are. Yes, it's true that marriage in the stepfamily is a package deal and you certainly can't separate the contents. However, in many package deals there's always one person who is the primary reason for the marriage and why the deal was consummated in the first place. That person is your major relationship and hopefully the person you will be staying with for a long time.

Kids come and grow. Eventually they will get married and leave you with each other or alone. Sometimes that is difficult to understand. For instance, we recall one client who was thinking about divorce for five years and couldn't leave. How could she leave her children? Every time she decided to leave, her parents and friends would say something like "you can't leave your children at six, eight, ten, or twelve years of age." It can be devastating (there is nothing like a good support system!). She went through marital, family, and individual therapy. She talked till her mouth ran dry. One day she quietly came into our office and said, "You know, living with someone you don't love is like being in a prison cell. I'm sentenced to boredom and hostility. My kids are going to grow up, leave me, and be okay. I can't wait around 10 years for them. It just isn't fair." She finally had made a choice.

Just like choosing your partner is important, choosing to keep your relationship as the primary focus of your family is ultra-important. We believe stepfamilies fail because marital relationships fail. Don't let your kids get in the way of your marriage. Even when life with the kids seems like hell on earth, keep loving your partner. If you really love and care for each other, the kids will come around. Sometimes, even more than you think. We'll talk more about this in later chapters.

When you look at the beginning of the relationship and at dating, single parents wanting to start a stepfamily have a tough time. Most custodial single parents are women and this is usually prescribed by law. Things are changing but very slowly. Many women believe that finding a man who is willing to marry a woman with children is difficult. They're right, it is. But even more so *if* you believe that nobody wants you. A lot of these women put the kid first in the relationship and then *him* second. That's pure disaster. Right from the start, it has to be you and him, not the kid, him, and you. Keep your mind on your priorities. You have developed a relationship with your child. Now work on a relationship with him and secondly with him and your child.

In any case, it's important that you work on developing a romance with your partner. Keep your child out of it for a while. The length of time is up to you but make sure that you have a good understanding of each other before you get your children involved. Get a babysitter. Have candlelight dinners. Go to the drive-in. Let yourself loose again! And, most of all, talk. Discuss your life together, expectations, goals, attitudes, values, and finally, family. Let this person know your children before he or she meets them. Make the path a little clearer for all those involved. Be on a firm footing before you subject yourself to any unnecessary torture. If you have a strong beginning relationship, you can avoid many of the hassles which will beset you. All parties concerned will need some adjustment in order for things to function properly. Many times you will feel like a bouncing ball between two sides, but in most cases, you will have to side with your partner to keep a family together.

Start this attitude right from the beginning. If this person is serious about you, having developed a love and caring between you will help things with the children. Believe us, you have plenty of love to go around and there will be enough for everybody. And, if you want to start right, develop a love with the special someone and side with him or her. After all, that's who you'll be sleeping with every night. That's the person who will understand you best of all. Keep them always in mind. Your children will respect you for that. After all, they will probably get married, too. Kids are important, but never as important as your marriage relationship.

When you are dating, the kids will express opinions about what you're doing. Often, jealousy will become involved. "How dare you spend time with so and so when you should spend time with me?" "How dare you go to that place without me? You know I wanted to go." "You do all the fun things with him."

Sometimes the remarks can be less tactful, "I think he's a creep." "She's really ugly, how could you go out with her?"

Kids are often good at playing with your guilt feelings. Remarks like, "Are you going to bed with him!" or "He's not like Daddy" or "I can't talk to her" can help you feel terrible. Kids can be cruel and yet at the same time be very loving.

Most of all, let's not forget that kids aren't adults. Generally they are self-centered, selfish, and immature. They believe the world is just for them and that they deserve everything and everyone. That's why adults tell people who are being immature that they're acting like kids. Kids have to learn to be adults and to practice loving and sharing with others, and parents are teachers and the role models. Don't expect your kids to be doing cartwheels just because you've found the love of your life. I'll never forget when Maggie told our kids that I loved her and that we were serious about each other. The kids screamed and cried. They told me I was a creep and to get lost. What a welcome! I thought, "What the hell am I getting into?"

That's when I realized a most difficult step and one we have repeatedly seen in stepfamilies. Often children will accept the "beau" as a friend. It's when things move past friendship into a possible Mom or Dad that the welcome wagon starts heading out the door.

Conversations like the following can ensue:

Child: You mean you're serious about that creep. She's awful!
Parent: Well, she was okay a week ago. You said you liked her then.

Child: Yeh, but you didn't love her then. I don't really like her.

Parent: What don't you like about her? (You're asking for trouble here.)

Child: Well, she's too bossy. She's not like Mom is, and she never pays enough attention to me. She's always talking to you.

Parent: Well, she likes you. She thinks you're neat (convincing will be a waste of time).

Child: Yeh, well I don't like her. (Child leaves and slams door.)

Adults often forget the insecurities and resentment that occur during this time for children. For instance, whenever Sally has her steady over, her Johnny sits right in the middle of them. Asking him to move is like displacing a brick wall. When he is put to bed, he screams and yells all night. Johnny is doing his best to keep Mom all to himself. Or the case of Susie who drinks scalding hot tea and screams, falls down, and does anything to get attention when Dad is entertaining a potential mate. Susie thinks she is the only woman in Dad's life and she'll try her hardest to ensure that.

We're not saying that all kids are unaccepting of a new Mom or Dad, but for most families this is a very difficult point. It just gets to be a complicated mess. A lot of times adults can see through kids, and even though they act and talk like they despise us, we still see a little love there. The problem is that as adults (just like kids), it gets hard to continually give love without a return. Sometimes a beau wants to give gifts to the children--maybe out of caring, or because he or she wants to bribe a child. Our belief is that gifts are not ways to build relationships. Time together with a child is better to us than

<u>any</u> material object. If you care for a child, spend time together. Relationships can't be bought. If you give a gift, save it for a special occasion and not as a regular habit.

You wonder after a while why you're hanging in there. This is an important growing point for the couple. Your mate needs to be extremely reassuring and helpful at this time. No matter what the kids say, stick up for him or her in front of them. You can talk about differences later. Remember, too, that the children may drive your beau to the point of outward frustration. Eventually, there may be some fireworks. In reality, those fireworks are pretty typical. Bob, a first-time parent, reacted like this and ended up spanking Darlene's five-year-old son when they were dating.

"I felt so embarrassed that it happened," he quietly related. "Joey just kept on pushing me, was rude, and called me names. One day he just hit me out of anger. It was at that time that I set a limit and spanked him for his behavior. It was kind of crazy after that. Darlene stood up for me even though Joey cried up a storm and blamed me for being a mean person. After that, Joey respected me and we are very close now."

As an adult and future stepparent, a person has to take a stand. Even if the kids profess to hate you, it's important that they respect you. There is no reason for you to be treated unfairly. The subtle behavior or the "I'll do it alone" posture may continue, but the hostile overt actions must be controlled.

If you take charge of the situation from the beginning, the journey will be easier. Relationships take time and you have plenty of that. But there is no reason that you can't be treated in a civil manner.

When things are getting too uptight, call a pow-wow. Sit down and share with each other. As adults you need to show caring and firmness. You also have to stick together as a couple and set a standard that will endure during your marriage. Courtesy, civility, and caring are a part of your family. Starting with these "C's" will help set a strong foothold for success. Later on in the book, we'll discuss how to expand upon the "C's" when you are in the early stages of establishing a committed family.

But let's be honest; kids have insecurities, too. They're as scared as you are. Most probably they have seen one parent leave. They've experienced loneliness and hurt. And they owe an allegiance to their other parent. They believe that it is akin to betrayal to like and love someone else. Our culture puts a restriction on love. We don't have enough love in us to care for two Moms or Dads. Sounds crazy, but people believe it! And relatives and friends help reinforce the idea. Even if your biological parent is not even near as good a parent as your "stepparent," he or she is still your only Dad or Mom. We know that fighting these myths can be hard. But we have seen them beaten. Kids can love immensely. They can give to you more than you can imagine. But it takes perseverance and work.

The custodial parent, while building the other partner up, also has to listen to the children's complaints and conflicts. Children almost certainly will make the custodial parent divide allegiance between the stepparent and biological parent. Our advice is to stay out of this triangle as much as possible. But if you have to make a decision, stick with the person to whom you are married. You may feel sorry for the other person and guilty, but if you choose the other way, your family will eventually disintegrate. You are starting a new family, stick with your future and not your past. This again can be difficult for the woman who still is taking care of the men in her life. We often see this phenomenon occurring where the woman just won't let go. Some people like to act married even after they're divorced. It helps keep the guilt down. Sometimes taking care of your ex-spouse feels good. But eventually, you must choose a side if your new family is to succeed.

The kids won't fully trust the new parent until they are sure the couple is committed. They have too much to lose. Why get involved and give your love if the marriage won't make it? That investment of love and time won't be given till a security exists for the children. In other words, the married couple creates that security by their love and respect for each other.

Another major impedance in the stepfamily is the children's investment in the other biological or non-custodial parent. Usually this person is far from overjoyed at the thought of his ex-spouse getting married. This jealousy can be an intense experience. The sharing about how to raise the children and other parts of their lives may be suddenly vanishing. The communication with the ex-spouse was often about the children and now someone is taking that away. The stepparent naturally forces the "ex" away, and rightfully so, for the family's survival. However, this is not so agreeable to the biological parents. They still want to keep some involvement--maybe more involvement than is realized.

But the custodial parent (normally female) will eventually pull out as she defines allegiance. The jealousy of the non-custodial parent towards the stepparent may be exhibited in various ways that are both subtle and overt. Comments such as "he can never be your real Daddy," or "he's okay for a stepparent" have been made. Sometimes the children get subtle messages of parental hurt or sorrow if they are too happy or spend too much time with the stepparent. "They can never be as good as me" messages are difficult to forget. Another message we frequently hear is "I'm so lonely and desperate without you." As therapists, we have found it gets very frustrating when parents behave in a self-centered way and thereby hurt their children. In these situations, children start to become possessions and one parent tries to outshine the other. The children become pawns in a game where a child's perception of family can become distorted.

Unless the parent is an abuser, it does little good to increase the damage by telling bad things about a parent. The children will have a relationship and in this regard they have some say as to its depth. The arguments about who is a better parent lead nowhere. The main prerogative in this situation is to focus on your own family. No one can tell you how to run your family, though others may try. In the stepfamily, it is important to keep your involvement in your own family as deep as possible and let the other parent take responsibility for his or her own actions. You may not like what is done or how it's done, but usually the law gives the other parent some specific rights.

If there is one rule of thumb that we want to share, it is this: The more you let the other parent into your stepfamily, the greater the problems you will have in integrating your family. It is important to note that, generally, a custodial parent will have the children most of the time and in this stepfamily the stepparent will be able to have a good deal of time and share many experiences with the children. Take advantage of it. Don't spend your life dealing with the non-custodial parent and fulfilling his desires or wishes. Fulfill your own.

It is also interesting to note that your own parents may not be quite as accepting as you would like them to be. The divorce was at least comprehensible, but this stepfamily stuff is a little more difficult.

Often parents will side with the other biological parent, even if they hated him or her. They may also believe that love is a restricted commodity. Parents start asking questions like "Do you think she is a good parent? How does he get along with the kids?" The funny thing is, how are you supposed to answer these questions? No, actually he's horrible." "Oh yes, she loves to beat them." When you were married previously, nobody asked how good a parent you were. All they wanted to know was when you were going to have children.

First meetings of the family can almost have a "looking glass" effect. It's as if everyone is watching the stepparent be a "parent." Thumbs up or down. It's a phenomenon that is somewhat unique to the stepfamily. Parental acceptance also takes time, and even though approval is usually given, you can expect some subtle reluctance.

One of the things that contributes to parental hesitancy is the sudden blending of the family. In reality, the parents are given little time to build up for this new "family." After all, there is no real honeymoon. Most couples sit around for years (or at least nine months) and talk about having children. Planning what they are to do, what to name their children, and what to buy. Friends and relatives are all a part of the ceremonial culture. With the stepfamily, none of this occurs.

You may hate the names of the children. All of a sudden, you are thrown into the situation. If one parent had been single, the circumstances can be even more threatening. It is not as if you had seen them since the day they were born. Rather, it's seeing them at whatever stage you appropriately land in. They could be throwing up at dinner or screaming like a teenager at breakfast.

Instantly, you have become a parent. All those rules you previously learned about a family come to a test. And unlike other families, you don't have the time to work out differences before the kids are born. You hassle as they stand around gloating at your misfortunes (and disagreements). You not only have to worry about yourselves as a couple but also about the adjustments the kids must make in order for the family to have a sense of stability. Through it all, try to keep a semblance of sanity and hold these suggestions in mind:

1. Keep your relationship first. If you have problems, talk about them. Don't argue in front of the kids if you can help it. Arguments give a chance for the children to believe the marriage will break up. Often they'll choose sides with the custodial parent to help the stepparent feel like a failure. Stick up for each other and fight in your bedroom.

2. Try not to go two different ways at once. Concede to the other person every once in a while. Compromise is the key to success. Iron out your disagreements. Don't let matters go unsettled for days and days; come to an agreement and stick to it.

3. Remember that everyone wants to say something about your lifestyle. Forget most of it.

4. If ex-spouses hassle you, agree with them and immediately forget what they said. Try not to spend half your life talking about your ex-spouse. Remember you are not married to that one anymore.

5. If the kids hassle you, talk to them and stick by your partner. Good listening is an art. Getting caught in the middle leads to heartache.

6. Above all, give love, reinforcement, and lots of positive strokes to each other. Believe us, you'll need it.

The Effects of the Ex-spouse
on Remarriage

Now that you've decided to get married, you figure your problems will decrease. Instead, they may escalate. And this can be very hard for couples to understand. One of the things we have learned from counseling people is that problems may get worse before they get better. People are usually resistant to change and so the fight is to stay the same or get worse. That's why, when parents try to change the behavior of a child, the behavior gets worse and <u>then</u> it gets better. If change were easy, everybody would do it.

One difficulty in your new marriage may be your relationship with your ex-spouse from your old marriage. No matter what shape your relationship was in (good or terrible), the odds are that the ex-spouse will try to help it get worse. There are many reasons for this if you take some time to think about it. For instance, the ex-spouse may be

- jealous because you've found someone else, even if he or she had no intention of ever having a relationship with you

- angry because the relationship with you and the kids is changing because of a new person on the scene
- confused because the new parent is taking away some responsibilities reserved for the ex-spouse
- resentful because the new person may be a better parent or better person (especially because this person has you!)
- upset with the children because they like the new parent
- lonely because now you have broken the final bond of a marital relationship by getting married.

Changing the relationship between you and the ex-spouse will not be easy, but it will have to come about if you are to be successful in your remarriage. You will have to formulate a new agreement that may not be satisfactory to all involved but will be mutually beneficial and healthy. In other words, what is healthy for each person may not be liked by everyone. In fact, some people like things to stay unhealthy. The purpose of the chapter is to explore more ways to begin that process of healthiness in your new relationship.

As you look at dealing with the ex-spouse, problems may start from the beginning. It may seem crazy but some folks ask their ex-spouses if it's okay to get remarried, or do you approve of the person, or what do the kids think? If you base your decision on other people's needs, we believe you really are in trouble. The one person who should make a decision about getting married is you. In reality, no one else matters. Even if your ex-spouse or your kids hate this new person, it is not their decision. Look at their intentions behind what they say. Nobody likes breaking up the status quo, so you might as well expect some hassle. Of course, it would be nice if everyone gave you their blessing, but this may not be the case. It boils down to you believing that the decisions you make in life are valid and that you want to be married to this person. When you rough the pros and cons, your happiness should have the most weight.

So, let's assume your ex-spouse doesn't like the remarriage and thinks you're an awful person for doing such a dastardly deed. So how do you work through this? One way is to state your feelings on the topic: "I'll listen to your opinion, but I also have mine, and since I have to live with this person, you'll just have to grin and bear it." Sounds easy but it's often hard to say those words. It's hard for us to stick up for ourselves. Sometimes feeling sorry for ourselves is a lot easier and less painful for the present moment. Our learning is that if you don't deal straight from the beginning, your problems will get even worse.

June, an administrative assistant in an oil company, felt terrible and happy about getting married at the same time. "Ron doesn't approve of the marriage and he has the kids siding with him. The thing that makes me so angry is that Ron never approved of anything I did anyway. He is so damn controlling. That's why I left him. I had a boss at work and I didn't need one at home. But I still seek his approval. And now the kids act just like him. He says it will ruin the children. I'm amazed that he is so interested in the kids now. When we were married, he worked half the time and watched television the other half. I had to beg him to do things together as a family. Now I have a man that really loves me and I think he'll be a good father. I guess they'll all have to learn to live with it."

So even if you have established that you are going on with your life, breaking a lot of old and painful ties, and finally making a life of your own, expect a lot of misery from others for doing it. One thing we've learned from working with families is that change is hard and usually doesn't get a whole lot of support. This may be particularly true of the ex-spouse.

The reaction of the ex-spouse may be subtle or overt manipulation. Common messages are: "Oh here you go; another failure." "You don't think the kids will accept that jerk, do you?" There may be threats of reducing child support or taking the kids away in a custody battle. In most cases, these are empty threats. And even if they are true, those threats could be carried out at any time that manipulation or control was needed and not just necessarily right now. If that's true, you might as well get it done. Not being lawyers, we are not in a position to give expert legal advice. However, it doesn't take a lawyer to figure out that if support isn't being received for a child, then the nonpayer may forfeit the right to see the child. Issues like these are worth discussing with a lawyer. The legal profession can become quite important to the stepfamily. Advice can be sought for many issues including parental rights, child support, visitation, and even adoption. Legalities often become the battleground of the stepfamily. Make sure you know your legal rights.

Manipulation by the ex-spouse may also be more subtle, particularly when it involves the children. Often this parent will attempt to gather forces and pull the children on his or her side. This can stir things up quite dramatically and usually starts a good argument. Our belief is that these arguments are a waste of time. One thing that you will learn quickly is that you cannot control what your ex-spouse does, particularly when he or she is with the children. During those times, this person is the parent and there is nothing you can do about it. So, arguing about how "things should be" or "how lousy you are as a parent" is useless. More often than not, you probably <u>never</u> agreed on parenting. Why start now? The chances are less than one in a million that you will come to terms on how to raise the kids, so why fight the battle? It will be a losing cause in the end. If you couldn't agree on how to raise kids while living in the same house, you certainly won't agree now that you're separated.

It may be true that the ex-spouse can bring the children to his or her side. "Isn't Mom awful because she is getting remarried and spoiling our family?" "I don't think Dad should remarry, because life will be miserable for you kids." Yes, it's amazing how adults can draw children into the middle of adult battles but it is also rather selfish.

We believe if you've got a problem with an ex-spouse, deal with this person directly. Try to keep from <u>using</u> the kids as messengers or receivers of anger that isn't their fault. Most ex-spouses are afraid of talking to each other truthfully and so they play the same games they did during their marriage. If they were jealous of the other person during the marriage, the jealousy continues.

George, a car salesman, fell into this trap. "I don't know how all this started. I admit that I was resentful of Lisa getting remarried. And so I started belittling her and Dick. Pretty soon the children got in the act. Everyone was carrying tales back and forth and it really got out of hand. So much damage has been done that Lisa and I barely talk to each other."

Many issues between ex-spouses focus on "control." Another term for this is "trying to run the other person's life." When you want to control somebody, it means you just can't let go, and if you're going to make it in a stepfamily, you're going to have to let go of your ex-spouse.

These "control" relationships can be disastrous. For instance, let's look at Suzie, the helpless ex-spouse. She calls all hours of the night for numerous petty chores. Common phrases are: "The plumbing doesn't work," "My car won't start," and "I can't discipline Johnny so he needs to talk to you." Most males feed on this ego-stroking and yet get angry at the same time. This type of woman will haunt you forever if you let her. It's like having two marriages at once and your new spouse will resent it. You probably left her because she is helpless and you're keeping her that way.

Another example: Mike, the nonchalant ex-spouse. He never seems to make a child support payment on time, if at all. However, he's quick to demand his rights and comment on your lifestyle and what his child needs in a home life. He might even make demands at any time, such as: "I will see my child today." If you listen to this person, you might as well be married to him.

We call this getting stuck in the biological trap. Because someone is the biological father, he can do anything and still have the privileges of being a parent. In other words, he can forget child support and still take the kids out for ice cream. We believe parenting involves both the good and the bad. If you can't help support the child, you don't deserve the relationship.

Joe, the sad ex, is a different story. His life is just "over" since you left and took the kids. He manipulates and has you drive 2,000 miles to drop off the kids because he's heartbroken without them. Whenever the kids come home, it reminds you of a funeral march. Everyone's crying and feeling bad for the poor ex-spouse who just can't seem to get his life together. With this person, a year's supply of antidepressants might be a good birthday gift. Don't be surprised if this person suddenly gets married without telling anyone. Depressed people are often pretty self-centered.

It may be apparent from our viewpoint that people are entitled to make choices in their lives. They can choose to live to the fullest extent or drown in their own misery. No matter what another person says or does, individuals must make their own choice of how to live.

You cannot make anyone feel or act or do in any way but what they ultimately choose to do. Trying to control people's lives and forcing them to do what you want is a useless waste of time and energy. All your yelling, screaming, persuading, and manipulating usually are for naught.

This is much easier to understand than it is to "do" with your ex-spouse. You may have a hundred things you want him to do and he just never seems to get your message. And the problem is that many books and professionals give strong advice to keep "in touch" with your ex-spouse, parent together, talk together, etc. Our reaction is that if you do this you may be heading for trouble and heartache. It just keeps those "I'm a creep" or "You're a creep" feelings alive and strong. You can't make a relationship work if you're not working on it regularly. And that is why so many relationships with ex-spouses fall flat on their face. Everything is going against it working. Divorce is a lousy hassling process that helps two people get angry at each other. You probably had trouble communicating when you spent every night together, so why should it get better? Many times you feel like getting revenge, so you hassle the other person till you get a reaction. Other times, you realize that you have devastated someone's life and that person is so lonely that you feel like crying when you see him or her!

Let's face it, for most of us it's just too painful to keep an involved relationship even if it sounds wonderful. We want to forget as fast as possible. Our bodies and our minds just can't take it. Most of us just want to move on. Remember the good times and moments you shared. Yes, I failed. Yes, it was a mistake. I wish I could start all over but I can't. And every time you see your ex-spouse all those feelings well up inside of you. Who needs all this pain? If my ex-spouse chooses to feel sad or mad at me for what has happened, so be it. But I've got to move ahead. I've found somebody else and I'm going to give it a try. Thinking about my ex-spouse is not going to help my present situation. I've got enough problems trying to get my family together to worry about my ex-spouse. You straighten out your own life, my friend.

Karen found this hard to do. "Everything I read said to keep a relationship with Larry. But the truth is I couldn't talk to him anymore. First, because he ran off with another woman and secondly, we had nothing in common. Our conversations were so superficial and boring that I just avoided them. The more I saw him, the better I felt about not being married to him. Being a friend meant I had to be close to him and I just didn't think it was worth my time."

From our viewpoint, in order to make a stepfamily work, two major tasks regarding the ex-spouse and you must typically happen:

1. Stop controlling your ex-spouse and let this person live his or her own life.
2. Concentrate on your new family and devote all your "family" energy to that task and not all those old messages.

These two factors are not separate entities and many times are intertwined. For instance, if your ex-spouse is taking up a lot of your time and thoughts, your new family will suffer. And probably your new spouse will be upset and angry. Nobody likes to hear about old spouses, particularly if they are infringing on your time with your new spouse. It's bad enough that the kids are a reminder of him or her. In most cases, reminding your new spouse of past relationships is a waste of time and energy.

Think about it from the stepparent's viewpoint. If this person likes the kids (and usually that's true), he or she has enough trouble developing a relationship with the children without having a spouse discuss an ex-spouse. For instance, it may be Mom talking about how things used to be with dear old "Dad." The kids just chime right in because it gives them the opportunity to feel sorry for themselves (and maybe get more goodies) or is an excuse to avoid getting close to their stepdad. So when you include the ex-spouse into your new family, you are helping your family not to grow. Add to this the concept of child support and the ever constant reminder of that money in your family and you have a typical stepfamily "touchy" situation. Because any stepfamily knows that no matter how much child support is, it doesn't pay the majority of the expenses which make a family function. So the stepdad ends up having quite an investment in the family--physically, emotionally, and economically. He may get to take in all the hardships of being a Dad without any of the rewards.

Mom is also put in a difficult position. She has to set the pace for family unity. And that means some sadness for her. In other words, for Mom to make the family work, she's got to pull out of the old family system. And we're talking about possibly two years of hard work and maybe longer. It means not getting involved in what the kids do with the ex-spouse, limiting discussion about him, putting a halt to "wonderful reminiscing," and standing up for "stepdad" when things get tough. We're not saying you can't talk to the kids about some experiences, but you have to let the children know they have two lives: one with him and one with you. And that's the way it will always be. He's a nice fellow but so is your new husband. Life moves on and you make the best of what you have as a new family.

This, of course, is easier said than done. There are several reasons for this. Many times it is easier to live in the past and keep from committing to a present relationship. Other people use the image of the ex-spouse as an angel that the new spouse must live up to. "So and so did this and you are never as good." The kids may also be resistant to establishing a relationship with the stepmom or dad because they feel like they are betraying their other parent. Children can keep and develop many relationships and yet adults are afraid to share this with them and understand their fears and insecurities. Giving children the freedom to love may be the greatest gift of all.

Another hassle we have seen is letting the ex-spouse pull you into a relationship with him and the kids. Sort of making it like old times. Instead, maybe conversations should be short and to the point. If the kids are dropped off at home with him standing around, maybe you shouldn't be there. This may sound cruel, but if the children believe you are interested at all, then they will believe you will get back together again or that there is no need to get involved in the present family. This could be very costly to you and your mental health. If you strongly desire a relationship with your ex-spouse, wait a few years. It will be a lot easier to manage. Trying to establish a relationship in the beginning of a new marriage can be detrimental and literally too time consuming. We feel that new marriages need to devote time to making the relationship work and not worrying about past problems. Every relationship needs to establish a comfortable understanding between the couple and this comes by spending time getting to know each other and not bothering with ex-spouses and their opinions, habits, whatever.

Another important point concerns the paying versus nonpaying spouse in regard to child support. Our philosophy on this point is fairly clear. If an ex-spouse doesn't contribute to their upbringing, he or she doesn't get to see them. Being a parent also means being supportive! It's a workable adage in life that states, "If you don't contribute your share, you don't reap the rewards." Nonpayment also creates great resentment on the part of the paying step-father. Why should the ex-spouse get the "jolly" times with the young (or children) without the hard work?

With the nonpaying ex-spouse, an alternative may be adoption by the stepparent. In other words, if you don't make a certain number of payments, you forfeit your legal rights. Many children who are adopted in the United States are members of stepfamilies. It's more than a matter of coincidence. Often it's a matter of family survival, stability, and choice.

Another influence on the stepfamily is the male who is paying for two families. This means he is living in one and paying child support in the other. Usually this person can't find a way out of this potential nightmare. His present wife complains that he gives too much money away and spends more than enough time with his "other" children. His ex-spouse says he spends too little time with their children and doesn't give her enough money. Either way, he's stuck.

If this situation is to succeed, the male must make his priorities known to his present family. No matter how hard he tries, he cannot spend all the time he wishes with them. Financially, the burden is harder. All the children need his support but not all the wives. He should attempt to do the best for his children but must realize the ex-spouse will use the money as she wishes and sometimes not as he wishes. Try not to be influenced by sad stories of financial incompetence. If the custodial parent can't afford the children, seek legal action to gain custody.

It is also important that the new wife accept the children from the past marriage just as you accept her children. Even if they are part-time visitors, each person (including parents) deserves respect and caring. Everyone must make an effort if the family is to succeed, and the adults are the persons who will set this example.

Peggy insisted on this concept from the beginning. "I knew the kids would have a tough time accepting me. Their mother hated me and told them so. Of course, Kenny's two girls weren't thrilled either about their Dad marrying another Mom. But I demanded that I be treated cordially from the beginning and Kenny stood up for me. If the kids were rude, he told them to straighten out. I always treated them with respect too, and I never put down their mother. Eventually the girls grew to like me and actually confided in me more than they did her. I guess you could say we worked it out."

Integrating the Family

We concede that the first few months of a remarriage and stepfamily are going to be tough. It takes perseverance, strength, love, honesty, positive manipulation, and caring for the marriage to work. One word may stick out from all the words and may seem like it doesn't belong ... MANIPULATION! We believe that this is probably the most important word of all. Think about that for a moment. We feel every human interaction involves manipulation. As therapists, we manipulate people to do "better" for themselves every time we are with them. Manipulation for positive growth, and that's what you as an adult need to do. Manipulate for the success and happiness of your family.

One problem we see with disturbed or unhealthy families is that the children are in control, not the parents. When that happens, you have big trouble. We teach parents how to gain control and manipulate. If someone is going to steer a ship, we hope it's an adult rather than a 10-year-old child. We're not saying you have to be a demagogue who rules with an iron fist. Rather, you are the director, or choreographer, who leads the family in the most positive direction. And that's what this chapter is all about. We're going to talk about keeping away from some costly mistakes which can cause you pain and suffering, two qualities most of us can use in lesser amounts.

In the beginning of a stepfamily, take for granted that there will be problems with the children. Even if life is a picture book story with love emanating in all directions, there will still be problems. Identity struggles, past family patterns, power struggles, and many other circumstances will occur. The children may deliberately or unconsciously use the turmoil to get their way and what they want. Kids can also be good manipulators but are somewhat narrow in their needs.

Billy was a good example of a child in need. When his Mom remarried, Billy thought that he wasn't getting the same amount of attention that he was used to. Soon he discovered he could get all the attention he needed by misbehaving. The one thing he noticed that got his mother extremely upset was to hassle her at dinner time either by not eating, throwing a tantrum, or refusing to feed the animals at supper time. Billy was manipulating Mom for his own needs and wasn't considering anyone else. Inadvertently, Mom was reinforcing his behavior.

When Mom called us on the phone, we decided to call a family conference. After we discussed why Billy was behaving as he did, it became easier for both parents to understand. We discussed a plan of action, talked about everyone participating, and insisted that the parents stick together. First, we decided that if Billy couldn't feed the animals, he couldn't eat either. In other words, if the animals weren't fed before he sat down for a meal, then he didn't have dinner.

Secondly, if Billy didn't eat or misbehaved, then he missed that meal. That also meant no snacks in between meals (which he pleaded for) because he must wait for the next meal. This was difficult for the parents because they thought they were killing their child by starvation. However, they soon found out that children are very active and waiting hours between meals got to be tiresome, and so Billy soon learned to eat on time with everyone else. Of course, Billy wasn't getting all the attention either, because he would leave the table and the parents could have a quiet dinner together (even though Billy tried to get noticed in every way imaginable).

Lastly, we talked about showing attention to Billy in a positive way and how to encourage him to do better rather than to discourage him to misbehave. Everyone likes to be noticed, and so we worked with the parents in learning how to recognize good and useful behavior. Billy enjoyed this, and he soon recognized that healthy behavior was more recognizable by his parents and more rewarding for him.

When we work with stepfamilies, we find that many have trouble establishing a family identity. Creating this so-called "identity" can be difficult and entails much work. It also requires investment on the part of the adults and, eventually, the children. A typical stepfamily in America involves a female single parent with children who marries a non-custodial male with children. Often the male will visit his children or the children visit him, but in that case they are only part-time family members. Sometimes these part-time kids have a role that is minimal, others more so, and yet at times they can be a disrupting force. We're going to spend most of this chapter talking about the beginning of the stepfamily unit.

To us, parenting in the United States is in a state of confusion and uproar. Even in the nuclear family, parents are having a tough time of it and not sure exactly what to do with their children. This state of upheaval in our culture creates an even more difficult situation for the stepfamily and requires that the parents stick together and work from one solid base of discipline. Hopefully, parenting has been discussed before you get married and, like most couples, you agree until the situation occurs and then you suddenly start to yell at each other. We forget sometimes that parenting involves many values, traditions, or experiences that make up this complicated task.

Lisa and Hank argue constantly over the kids. "Hank says I'm too easy on them," Lisa remorsed. "I just feel like they have been through a difficult time and I don't want to cause any trouble for them. They get to see their real father only once a month. I just feel bad that I've hurt them so much."

Hank disagrees with the philosophy. "I know the kids have been through a tough time, but that's how the world is. We've got to be doing things around here and all everybody does is think about the past. I'm getting tired of it."

Hank and Lisa each have very good points, but their disagreements are not helping the children. In these situations, the children can become depressed, act out, or constantly harass the parents.

When you think about it, first-marrieds have the blessing of a year to build up a relationship, and time for intimate discussions about their child and how they are to discipline Suzy or Johnny. Many times, they have been married for several years and have worked at establishing communication between themselves and will use this as a base with their child. Even so, most couples find parenting to be a most hazardous profession. The stepfamily has no such luxury. Thrust into establishing a marriage and trying to make it work, the last thing they may want to do is worry about kids. Besides struggling with their own identity as a couple, they must also come to terms with being parents and a family.

All this struggle becomes intertwined and sometimes you feel like screaming. If you don't start out on the right foot with all of this, you certainly will be a step-family ... out of step and always a step behind. Conflict will follow you everywhere.

Mary, an insurance executive, got tired of the hassle. "My kids would never accept Tom, and I found myself calling up my ex-husband, Ken, for help with the kids. When I talked to a therapist about my problems, I mentioned that Tom seemed to be avoiding everyone. It suddenly dawned on me that I was creating the distance. I was used to calling all the shots and when I couldn't I'd ask Ken, who usually didn't help much anyway. I guess it just felt good to talk to him. I realized that I was keeping Tom out of the relationship. It made sense for me to begin my new family rather than to live in the past. If the kids wanted to do that, then it would be their problem."

How do each of the family members feel about the stepfamily? The male may have numerous feelings. He knows he loves his wife and yet has mixed feelings about the new children. Torn in conflict, he expects the wife to support him at all times, particularly in troubling circumstances with the children. Sometimes she does not do this. This creates anger within him and separation both from his wife and the children. He likes the kids and at other times resents them. As a stepfather, he does all the things a father does without the rewards. He attempts to discipline and feels sabotaged from all sides. He may not only be financially supporting this family but also the other children from a previous marriage. This man may end up penniless and yet nobody thinks he's okay as a person.

Tom related his feelings about this. "Susan and I disagree on how to discipline the children. I think she is too soft and so I speak up when I think the kids misbehave. When this happens, she sticks up for them and not for what I say. So, we end up having a big fight and the kids do whatever they want. She keeps on telling me she'll support me <u>next</u> time, but it never happens. However, she gets angry when my kids come over for the weekend and screw up. Then it's my fault because I don't discipline them enough. It's getting to the point where I'm just tired of it." It seems like Tom and Susan are pitted against each other and the family is becoming the loser.

Sometimes, the kids are engaged in a different struggle than the parents. Feeling that Mom has betrayed them, they may resent this new father before he steps in the house. Judged guilty before even a trial has been set. Things will never be the same. He's going to take away our time with Mom. They are jealous that he gets to be boss just because he's an adult. It's like the kids are saying, "We'll break up this fling even if Mom's happy. Let's side up with Mom when they have fights, talk about all his faults, and start up struggles by disobeying and causing problems. We'll just do little things to get them annoyed." The kids may feel like they are traitors if they like this new man. So even if they like the parent, they may pretend they don't, rather than face up to feelings they would rather hide.

Mom gets more confused than ever. If she supports her ex-spouse, the kids get closer to her, but her new husband drifts farther away. If she does the opposite and pulls towards her new spouse, the kids get angry. She's always getting pulled from side to side. Wanting help with parenting, she rejects her new spouse's efforts because they represent change for her and lots of work. "I liked it better when it was buddy-buddy with the kids. Now it's back to parenting and that's hard." However, if he doesn't get involved, she'll lose both him and the kids. What a mess!

Linda used to think it would be easy. When Sam and her were dating, the kids liked him and even her ex-spouse said it was good for her. It was _after_ they got married that everything got tangled up. "I think it's a disloyalty problem," Linda shared. "The kids feel if they get close to Sam, then Lou will get upset. And Lou has helped reinforce some of that garbage. I think they can love Sam if they give him a chance and still love Lou. I believe that each person can be important to them if they would give it a chance. Instead, everyone keeps on blaming me for their problems. Sometimes I think they are all spoiled kids and I have to be the parent. That's probably a problem I have ... wanting to be in charge all the time and telling people what to do. Maybe they should just fight it out."

This is how the world turns for the stepfamily. Many people are confused about what to do and find that typical family responses help matters get worse. Advice from relatives and friends is mostly useless, and so you end up feeling confused and defeated. This is where chaos occurs and everyone goes in different directions.

We believe that for the stepfamily to work, structure is very important, particularly within the first few years. The parents must take charge by setting limits and guidelines as to how the family will function. These can be discussed with the whole family, but the parents must hold strong convictions if they are to succeed. When we work with families, we stress the following points:

1. Discuss parenting before you get married. If you forgot to do this, discuss it now! Hour-long discussions shouldn't be on the vague philosophy of parenting, but on the specifics or "how to's." Come to agreement on the many structures that are integral to the family situation. This means when we eat as a family, what time the kids go to bed, manners of speaking to adults and children, when T.V. is on, activities that are done together, how money is spent, what chores are shared throughout the house, and many other trivial items that get to be major affairs when rules are in chaos.

    We believe that kids take an active part in household chores when they are as young as five or six years old. This means without sex-stereotyping, either. In other words, five-year-old males can help wash dishes or load them in a dishwasher as well as seven-year-old girls helping wash the car. Our idea is not to frustrate kids, but to show them that life is full of work and play and usually not an extreme doing of one or the other. We believe that too many adults "protect" their children from being responsible in the honor of being a "good parent."

We give no lee-way on working out these rules between the parents. Many couples hee-haw around and refuse to come to a decision. To us, no decision is a decision not to act. You are deciding to let your family deteriorate in front of your very eyes. In the extreme, families without rules or inconsistent ones create crazy or disturbed family members. Adults owe their families proper consideration.

2. After rules are structured by the parents, sit down and discuss them with the children. Present them as a couple and as parents who know what they are doing. After all, you do know more about parenting than the children.

After you state the rules, listen! Open your ears for discussion and determine in your head if any rules need changing. Do not change rules right then and there. If there are changes, discuss them as a couple afterwards and make a joint decision. Children do have a contribution to make. However, they can also be self-centered and want to avoid any work or structure. This resisting will have to be examined by the parents and they must not give in to manipulation (crying, hassling, screaming, etc.). Remember, everyone is a procrastinator at one time or another.

When there's resistance, you must state that the rules go into effect immediately. If there is a deliberate choice of denial or disobedience, then there must be suitable consequences. We do not believe in physically hitting a child (although two-year-olds may require gentle tugging) but rather more natural consequences. For instance, if a child doesn't pick up his clothes, they don't get washed. If she doesn't show up for dinner, no food. If you don't wash the dishes, you eat from dirty dishes. Deliberate disobedience may mean restriction of privileges. We'll talk more about these specifics in a later chapter.

3. Learn to believe in the philosophy that families help each other. Teach your children to appreciate giving to one another. If a family is to succeed, you all must take part in the good or bad. That means chores are for everyone just as the rewards are. If both parents work (and who doesn't) the kids may have to help more than ever. It will help them in the long run, particularly when they get married. Kids usually adjust to these responsibilities fairly well, but sometimes parents feel angry and guilty. They get upset that sex roles are changing and also feel that they are neglecting their kids because they work. Economics dictate family changes, and moaning about spending less time with your kids does little good. Making the best use of your time is your best alternative. Use it thoughtfully!

Ophelia felt guilty about spending so much time away from the children. "I know we can't make it without my income but I still don't feel good about it. The kids are spending so much time in day care and I really miss them. But that is the way it is and so the time I do spend with them is precious. I'm finding that I value my time with them more than I used to and that I try to make the most out of each moment. Maybe I worry too much. After all, the kids seem to be getting along well."

4. Everyone must be committed to the concept of family if the stepfamily is to work. Each person must accept and be willing to work hard at loving the kids. When you get married everything is yours, including the kids. The mine-and-ours syndrome is what leads to divorce.

   Beyond commitment, there are words which signify togetherness. We strongly suggest that the stepmom or stepdad is called Mom, Mamma, or Mother, or Dad, Daddy, or Pop. Calling "people" by the title signifies commitment both by the parent and child. Calling the person by his first name, such as Joe, gives him the status of your mailman or gas station attendant. When you are supporting children and doing the job of parenting, you deserve the title. Children have enough love to give to three or four parents. They won't get too hung up on the title unless adults do. Yes, children may get angry at first and refuse. Yes, your ex-spouse might be jumping up and down. But change is hard.

   If you're a family with a Mom and Dad, then call yourselves Mom and Dad. As the children speak the words, they will establish what we call a "cognitive framework." In other words, if you say it long enough, you learn to believe it and it sticks in your head.

   And that also goes for the parents. Introduce the children as your children. "This is my son, Tom or daughter, Suzy" rather than "This is-uh-Carol's kid or uh-my stepdaughter."

Try to call yourselves Mom and Dad in front of the children. If they refuse to comply, keep after them. Eventually, it is worth the bother.

The people who have the most trouble with titles are usually adults. Adults have come to place great significance on names and yet do not realize their use within the family. The terms Mom and Dad mean involvement and commitment, values that many adults run from with a passion. Our advice is that if you don't want the title, don't marry someone with children. If you're in a stepfamily, you are a parent. Accept that fact. Even though this advice is hard to take or understand, we have found calling individuals by a name that denotes a family helps create a family. We are less insistent about this rule when children only visit for short periods of time (i.e., two weeks for the summer). However, if the stepparent is going to spend as much if not more time with the children then the ex-spouse, we believe it is fruitful to give the stepparent a parental surname.

Though hesitant at first, Bob agrees with this concept. "I felt uncomfortable at first when they called me Dad but I have to admit that I liked it. It was really Carol's idea and she supported it even over the kids' objections. It was funny, but after the awkwardness was over and we had sat down and discussed it, everyone felt better. In fact, I started to feel more like a Dad and the kids began treating me better."

5. The custodial parent must support the new parent at all times even if they disagree. This means sticking up for him or her (even if this person's wrong), letting this parent be a parent and agreeing, forcing the kids and this new parent to spend time together, talking about the new parent in positive terms, not getting stuck in the middle of arguments, forgetting about your ex-spouse and how it used to be, supporting the new parent and not the ex-spouse in front of the kids.

   Remember that this is your new family. Act like it's your last and that you're giving it 200 percent. If you disagree, discuss it in private. Above all else, never argue in front of the children when you are first married. Wait till you are settled and accepted before displaying this type of behavior in front of the kids. Arguing may scare them and remind them of the past divorce. The stepfamily needs stability and the custodial parent provides this force.

   The children will act out. They will be sad for the missing parent and complain how hard life is now. The new parent may want to run away and hide. The custodial parent is the glue of the family. Without your perseverance and strength, it won't stick.

6. When the non-custodial parent gets visitation rights and the children spend weekends or nights, they should live in the family by established family rules just like everyone else. Don't create new rules or allow rules to be changed because things are different somewhere else. Acceptance of the child is important, but this does not mean changing the family to

accommodate varying needs. Help the child to function within your family unit and not vice versa. Once you start creating new circumstances, you will be letting the child rule the family, and this is a mistake. The non-custodial parent usually feels very guilty about not seeing the kids and tries to make a party of it or attempts to get everyone to act like this is an extraordinary event. We believe that, instead of making it such a spectacular event, the non-custodial parent should show the child a normal family and spend special time talking with him or her. In the end, special time together will be more important to the child than any amusement park or present.

Establishing a Stepfamily Lifestyle

Now that you've established some guidelines for running your family, you may wonder what to do to establish a lifestyle. By lifestyle we mean a family that works together and respects each other's individuality. It is our contention that every family needs a healthy lifestyle. This is a challenging task indeed!

Much of your lifestyle is established through risk and change. For example, you may realize that the manner in which you parented in your past relationship just doesn't seem to work anymore. Maybe you need to be more positive or show more caring for the child. This is exciting but scary. A child could be in a similar situation. Maybe she never could show the affection she felt towards an adult and now her new father welcomes that affection. What an exciting experience for both of them! And yet it can be very hard.

Most of us want to change but lack the perseverance. It requires a commitment to follow through. Think of habits you've wanted to change and still do the same. Eat too much? Throw your shoes in the closet? Let others manipulate you?

For the male, getting in touch with feelings is sometimes a struggle. He may want to get close to others, but doesn't know how or is afraid to try. This may be especially difficult for him when he begins a stepfamily. He may want to show affection but these "are really not my kids." "How can I hold them when I have trouble caring for my own kids?" It's crazy, but this person is avoiding his natural impulse and instinct makes excuses for his behavior. "Oh, they would reject me anyhow." "I didn't want to confuse them."

Some men are stuck in the stepfather-lust situation. In other words, you can't love a female without lusting for her physical body. In a way, we admit that sexual intercourse is a natural phenomenon and a need for both sexes. However, we usually see it as detrimental when between father and daughter, but we have worked with families where it didn't damage either party.

But most of the time it does, and this is due to both family considerations and cultural needs. To us, this is a complex issue of which books have been written. In a brief way, we will explain our viewpoint.

To us, children need the freedom to be sexual in the family, particularly when a young girl is growing up and getting in touch with her sexual identification. Too many men do not understand this process and their wives don't explain it to them. So instead of understanding the female girl as "child sexy," they misinterpret it as "adult sexy."

And in turn the stepfather acts in his adult sexy way and thus takes the child beyond her "child sexy" to areas where she does not want to go or does not understand. Instead, the male needs to act in a parental sexy way, which includes the following:

1. Accept your child's sexuality and talk about it. People often use their own insecurities to avoid asking if their child understands "making love," their sexual organs, attraction to men, etc. If you are uptight about sex, your child will fear sex and thus be afraid of men or more susceptible to incest.

2. The father should be able to hold and kiss his stepdaughter in a caring and affectionate manner. However, it should be different from the way in which he holds and kisses his wife. With a child it should be more childlike.

3. A common fact known to therapists is that in families where there is incest, the mother is aware of the problem and chooses to ignore it. Usually this is because she is insecure or is not meeting her husband's emotional and sexual needs in the marital relationship. In other words, incest is a family problem.

A last situation to consider is the stepfather who moves into a family with a teenage child. There must be an adult understanding and agreement between husband and wife that the girl will be flirtatious, particularly with her "mother's mate." In a sense, then, competition should be more amusing than threatening. For the male it can be enjoyable if he understands what is occurring and maintains the marital relationship as an important priority. Private time and demonstrations of affection between the marital couple are very important with teenagers. Eventually, they will come to respect your relationship and find mates of their own. An open sharing between spouses about both feelings and behaviors between father and daughter can keep a natural occurrence from becoming a problem.

We understand that risk and change can hurt. A child may reject you or deliberately disobey you because of what you represent, not what you are. This may bother you, but we believe this type of pain can be helpful. Usually anything worthwhile in life involves some pain. It's just that you have to risk change and endure pain till you get some happiness. Sometimes this happiness takes effort and risk.

Beginning a remarriage and stepfamily is another chance for many individuals to make it right this time. It is a chance to become more fulfilled and to forget about the past. Concentrating in the here and now is a key ingredient to a successful lifestyle. Being positive towards life's circumstances and each other is another important attribute. Let's look at lifestyles in the stepfamily.

If there is one lifestyle that will dominate the road of the family, it is the couple's. In essence, they model the lifestyle for the children. They are in a position to show what a good relationship means and how to get close to another human being. This certainly does not mean that you are a couple of angels who make no mistakes. In fact, making mistakes and being human are very good qualities. It's just that the couple sets the tone for the marriage and is also the major relationship model for the children. Often people determine relationships based on the model their parents showed them. This can be very good or very bad. Many disorders of the human condition are passed down through families and if couples were better models there might be less alcoholism, child abuse, truancy, etc.

When we look at a marital relationship, good couples seem to have some common characteristics. Some of the most prominent values we see are these:

<u>Caring</u>: Other people call this love, friendship, and infatuations. The components are basically the same. Caring means showing persons that loved ones are special and not taken for granted. Maybe life would not be the same without them. Both sexes can reach out and touch or hug to show they care.

In successful remarriages, the partners can tell that their spouse is very important to them. They accept each other as they are but at the same time push for growth. They also enjoy a sense of humor and realize that life isn't such serious business. Sticking up for each other is a habit, not an effort. When they slander, they do it in private, not in public. They make a pact that nobody steps in between them.

In Jill's first relationship, things like this never happened. "We would yell at each other constantly and he always seemed to belittle me. His remarks were so cutting. I was just never good enough for him. My marriage with Tim is so much different. It was very important from the beginning that we respect each other. If either of us has a problem, we don't knock each other down but instead we sit down or yell or whatever we need to get it out of the way. Tim pushed for not arguing in front of the kids and I wholeheartedly agree."

Listening: This is a rare quality. It means both partners talk and each person is understood. It does not mean that there must always be agreement, but rather that each side has its say. Listening means recognizing that something is bothering your spouse and you're the one person he or she can talk to about it. It also goes the same way for those happy moments in life. Good listeners have a way of drawing people out so that conflicts can be resolved. It means taking time out each day to talk rather than sit and stare at a T.V. Each person is actively involved in the other's world and wants to hear about his or her day. These people don't mumble life away but feel free to talk because their message is heard.

This also means setting aside a time each day that is the couple's time for talking. It doesn't mean that a spouse has to drop everything whenever he calls. "You don't love me unless you talk to me right now" is a power-oriented motive that turns people off. If a person is busy, they have a right to finish a task. However, if this person keeps on avoiding you, it is time for a discussion.

Confrontation: Good relationships have a little flame under the cooking pot. If a partner upsets you, you let him or her know, gently but with vigor. There is no game- playing and storing up of old hurts like squirrels hide nuts in the winter time. No, everything is out front and hurts are discussed so they don't happen again. This is not the yelling and screaming many couples exhibit but rather an emotional and cognitive discussion. Both persons get to voice their opinion and overpowering by increased voice volume is diminished. Problems are shared when the mood is accepting rather than wanting to "get back" at the spouse.

It is our contention that couples need to be able to disagree. In fact, we are very wary of couples that never argue. It usually signifies that the relationship is dead. There doesn't always have to be a winner, because that means there's a loser. Instead, it's important that opinions are heard and that each person thinks about what the other has said. Maybe you can think it over for a few hours, days, or weeks. In the end, compromise will be the answer rather than competition.

Happiness: The couple enjoys life and realizes that misery passes and it is only a part-time thing. These folks can weather hardship and work their way through it. Even the hardest times have some fun in them. They realize that the happier they are, the more life brings pleasure. Enjoyment of each other is also a prime part of the relationship. Simple things in life can make these people happy because they realize each day is special and something to be shared together.

Wayne Dyer, in his book Your Erroneous Zones, aptly describes happy people as "those who like virtually everything about life--people who are comfortable doing just about anything and who waste no time in complaining or wishing that things were otherwise. They are enthusiastic about life, and they want all that they can get out of it. They like picnics, movies, books, sports, concerts, cities, farms, animals, mountains, and just about everything. They like life. When you are around people like this you'll note an absence of grumbling, moaning, or even passive sighing. If it rains, they like it. If it's hot, they dig it, rather than complain about it. If they are in a traffic jam, or at a party, or all alone, they simply deal with what is there. There is no pretending to enjoy but a sensible acceptance of what is, and an outlandish ability to delight in that reality."

<u>Sexuality</u>: This doesn't mean that each person is infatuated as in the early stages of a relationship but rather that there is still some excitement or electricity between them. They still hold hands, hug each other, playfully care for each other, and are not afraid to demonstrate affection in front of family members. In other words, they still find their partner attractive and sexually interesting.

<u>Individuality</u>: Even in all the togetherness, each person is an individual who has a separate life. Not every waking moment is spent together and each person is not actively trying to control the other. Jealousy is at a minimum since all persons believe in themselves. Statements like "You have to be in by ten," "Where were you? Spending another night with your friends?" are rare and seldom used. Each person can pursue his or her own path knowing that it contributes to each of them. However, major decisions are made with a spouse but ultimatums such as "choose this or choose me" are not stated. Rather, each person develops himself while caring for the other person.

Leo Rosten says it well: "We can never entirely understand someone else and each of us remains part stranger even to those who love us. It is the weak who are cruel; gentleness is to be expected only from the strong ... You can understand people better if you look at them—no matter how old or impressive they may be—as if they are children. For most of us never mature, we simply grow taller."

<u>Sharing</u>: Life and all its pleasures are shared. No horrendous secret or hidden bank accounts. With the modern dual career couple, the two struggle with doing their part and trying to understand each other rather than vying in a power competition. Responsibilities with the children are shared for life's enjoyments and hassles are a co-project.

In his book <u>Living, Loving and Learning</u>, Leo Buscaglin points out the need for sharing. "If we ever needed each other, we need each other now. Divorce rates are growing, relationships are casual and mostly meaningless. The suicide rate is doubling, especially among young people. Intimacy is not simple. It's a great challenge to our maturity. It's our greatest hope."

<u>Commitment</u>: These people do not seek satisfaction of major marital needs outside the marriage, for this causes eventual destruction.

They have the feeling that even if things are hard, they will give it their best shot and then some more. No backing out of this relationship. They don't use "I'm going to leave you" as a threat to coerce someone to do what they want them to do. There isn't a daily fear that this person can leave at any moment for the slightest reason.

On the other hand, parents and children share many of the same values. However, the adults are the parents in charge and carry a sense of responsibility for the child's welfare. A child also needs commitment in his relationship with parents.

Commitment may be the most difficult value for stepfamily members to share. Without it, family members will look outside the family for love. Family members need to be able to depend on each other in order to give and have a feeling of security. Unfortunately, parents may not understand that they need to develop and model this behavior before the children will come along.

<u>Unconditional Love</u>: Many parents get caught in a bind that sticks with them for all their life which they pass on to their children. It's called, "I love you if." The inherent message is that I only give you my love if you do things my way. Some examples are, if you're good, eat

your food, go to school, be a lawyer, be a mother, marry so and so, live near us, etc. The messages can go on forever. The sad thing is when the child believes them. Often they are combined with a guilt trip such as tears or sadness by the parent if you are not "just perfect."

If this is taken to the extreme, it can create a child that becomes crazy. These families give constant double messages to their child; a damned if you do, damned if you don't statement. Most of these are usually filled with guilt. An example would be a mother that says "Go out and have a good time. Don't worry about me staying here all alone and sad."

A more positive and healthy manner is to accept persons as they are. I love you because you are. This means separating what the parent terms "wrong" behavior from the person. In other words, sometimes the way you act or your behavior upsets me but I still love you as a person. This idea means that children need to see that you love them and that once in a while (like all of us) an "action" upsets you. The action does not make them unloveable. Somehow many kids learn that love is conditional and so this is what they eventually practice with their friends, relatives, and, eventually, spouses.

<u>Guidance</u>: Every child needs structure and discipline. In reality, through discipline you teach a child what freedom is. And, funny as it may sound, with freedom comes an "implied" responsibility. For instance, I may be free to drive a car in the wrong lane but my freedom will probably end rather drastically. There are rules of safety for all of us. Freedom and order go hand in hand. Letting a child have unrestricted freedom creates tyrants. Usually, the parents take up all the responsibility for this type of child and become angry. Meanwhile the

child wants everything his or her way and does not learn the guidelines and rules for societal and family living. Well-defined restrictions give a child a sense of security.

Each child needs structure and has to learn to participate. Much of this philosophy is shared throughout this book. We are saying that children need to make choices and voice their opinions. Listening to what they say is very important because they have many good ideas. We believe that if children are taught to participate from their early childhood, then they will want to contribute as they grow older. Whether you wish to admit it or not, most people (and children) like reaching a goal after it took some hard work. Those accomplishments by the child need to be appreciated. Too often, parents recognize the negative and ignore the positive. The converse would probably be more helpful.

Sacrifice: Children must realize that they are part of a family and that they have a share in the family's success. This means sacrificing for the good of others and learning that sometimes everyone has to give a little in order for all to gain. For instance, if Mom and Dad both work, then the children will have to do more chores without complaining. This may sound easier than it is. Often the parents have to sit down and explain what life's struggles are about. Sheltering children from reality teaches them that life is unreal. We're not saying that they have to be adults at the age of 10 but rather that they can grasp the idea of contributing their share of work. A myth in this idea is that all things will be equal. This is an ideal goal but it may be unattainable. Relationships are not 50-50 all the time and sometimes life is unbalanced. This is particularly true for children where the scales are rarely balanced in their favor when dealing with adults. Children should be treated as equal human beings, but they are not equal in regard to experience or life skills.

Learning to deal with being inexperienced and receiving guidance is a part of life that most people know and accept. Part of this involves learning sacrifice for others during that process. To take that away from a child is depriving the child of a marvelous opportunity.

The last major lifestyle bonds are important attributes needed between children in a stepfamily. Some of these include:

Cooperation: Siblings need to care and cooperate with each other rather than to compete all the time. This can be hard. Parents often inspire their children to be at each other's throats or to hassle one another. Cooperation is taught and is respect for others. A good way of doing this is to make children do tasks together where part of the task must be completed by each person and if it is not completed both (or however many) assume the consequences. Children can be taught to appreciate the good qualities in their siblings and that they can help each other through their troubles. They need to learn, be told and shown that brothers and sisters are special people.

Responsibility: Siblings need to learn to be responsible for self and for others. Rather than blaming problems on a sibling, the person must accept his own fate. Also, the young must come to value each other and protect each other from outside influences. It's important that siblings learn to care, love, and protect each other from harm. This can be modeled from parents.

Establishing an effective lifestyle for a stepfamily takes work, commitment, and cooperation. We believe that in any family the lifestyle and leadership of the marital couple provides the impetus for positive functioning.

It is important that the marital relationship is the primary focus for the couple and that the children develop from the strength of the relationship. If they can establish a lifestyle that teaches effective values for the children, then the family is on the road to being successful and fully functioning.

The marital couple has to understand that everyone might not be interested in helping this task. Parents, friends, relatives, ex-spouses, and children could be resistant to this idea. You have to be determined to overcome minor (and you may see them as major) obstacles. As a positive and caring lifestyle is established, the children will come along. We believe people would rather be happy and productive than looking at each day as a laborious task. Working on your lifestyle will help this task.

Old Memories and the Stepfamily

Besides having an influence on the children and their commitment to the family unit, the ex-spouse can also have a dramatic impact on the functioning of the marital couple. The real-life presence or the so-called "ghost" and past remembrances of the ex-spouse can cause such a rift between a couple that they may consider divorce as a solution to this problem.

This may be because the couple is not actually married since one spouse (or possibly two) is still attached to an ex-partner. This "connection" may be psychological, physical, or religious.

Some individuals will deny that an ex-spouse is affecting their marriage. Tony and Joanne were seriously considering divorce when they came for therapy. We quickly discovered that Joanne still loved her ex-husband and that Tony could never live up to his image. Tony was giving up and started to seek excitement and companionship outside of the relationship. They were fighting constantly, and yet we could see that each of them deeply cared for the other.

When we talked to Joanne, we discovered that she was in contact with her ex-husband several times a day, usually concerning the kids or the house. She rationalized that this was very necessary "since Tony never was around to help." The kids were aware of what was happening so they helped create a crisis each day so that Mom "could call Dad." Their wish was to get Mom and Dad together and it appeared to be working. The children helped start arguments between Tony and Joanne that had to do with "how Tony treated them." They were effective in pulling Mom on their side and thus everyone rejected Tony. After a while, Tony felt like a "stranger in a strange land."

After bringing this process into the open, Tony and Joanne started to work on their relationship. We confronted Joanne with the prospect that her ex-husband left her and had since remarried. It was unlikely that he would be coming back since he was happy. Joanne came to terms with her resistance to getting close to Tony because she was afraid "she would get hurt again."

On the other hand, we discussed with Tony the need to get more involved with the children and to spend more time at home.

We allowed the children to continue making daily crises but Tony was called by Joanne. In a short period of time, the crisis slowed down and this also allowed the kids and Tony to get closer.

The children saw their "Dad" whenever it was feasible but Joanne pulled out from between them and let the kids determine that relationship, not her. She also learned how to get close to Tony and to side with him in regard to the kids. With the barriers gone, this stepfamily started closer relationships.

Some of the reasons for conflict in a stepfamily are natural. When you have been in a serious relationship before, you often have expectations of what is to occur in a new relationship.

At times, you may expect your new spouse to behave like the old one. This is usually true when they don't behave as you would like them to do. Any person you live with is going to cause adjustments or changes on the part of both people. However, when you have already had an intimate relationship with someone you might have grown accustomed to certain attributes.

These attributes are normally the ones that make life more pleasant for us. "He was always so loving," or "She never forgets to cook dinner." Seldom do we say, "Oh, you don't yell as loud as him," or "It's a shame you don't lay in bed all day like her." All these thoughts and possible arguments usually can be traced way back to your past relationship. If anything haunts us in the stepfamily, it is our past. You must come to terms with it if you are to succeed.

Sometimes this is not easy. People can place their ex-spouses in places of adulation, especially if they were the one that was left behind in the relationship. Jim felt like he would never find anyone like his first wife. "I told my new wife that she could never replace Sally or be the mother that she was. Women like her are just very rare and I just have to admit that I'll never find another to take her place. Sometimes you have to settle for second best." Unfortunately second best is usually not good enough for most people.

In thinking about our ex-spouses, feelings are usually mixed. Parts of them we dislike, others we like; and yet, a good part of us would like to forget it ever happened. It's denial that can cause us the most grief and sadness. Denial of your past, your growth, and what you are becoming.

When we look back at most people in our past, most of us forget the worst and try to remember pleasant experiences. It is our mind's way of coping. If we dwell on the negative, our life becomes miserable and depressing. That's why children who are abused or women married to alcoholics will have memories of nice events. Even in traumatic events such as rape, the victim will often block out the circumstances in an effort to cope. The problem is that somewhere in our minds, events keep itching away until they are faced.

So, it is not hard to understand that you may like to remember a happy past when you think about your ex-spouse. Sometimes, you will even have difficulty telling children the real reasons that it ended. It's almost like you want to hide it in a shroud of mystery. Of course, the other extreme is the person who constantly criticizes the ex-spouse and admits that he or she is to blame for all of life's evils. This person is also having difficulty in facing the past but it's a different type of denial. But it is still denial.

Denying circumstances surrounding an ex-spouse can be damaging. For example, we find that clients have a tough time telling their children that "Dad and Mom" had to get married and that the relationship had trouble right from the beginning. On the other hand, these same parents are shocked if their 16-year-old daughter gets pregnant and wants to elope. Sometimes hiding secrets creates more secrets.

Another phenomenon that we find interesting with ex- spouses is that they can use their children as spies on each other. After spending time with a parent, the child is given a barrage of questions. Typical questions in the interrogation include these:

- Did he spend money on you?
- Who is her boyfriend?
- What did you do, eat, say?
- Is he going on a vacation?
- Is his girlfriend fatter than me? etc., etc.

The child is placed in the position of being an informer or maybe giving information that is of no business of the ex-spouse. Our rule is, "If you have a question, ask it yourself."

So, what is it that you are so afraid to face? What is it that keeps you from being free of the past? Usually, there are several reasons.

1. <u>If you admit your ex-spouse's faults, you must admit your own faults</u>.

    When you look at what your ex-spouse did, you usually had a part in it. That's why it's called a relationship. You act and react. It's all part of the intrigue of marriage. If he was "selfish," you may have reacted in many ways. Maybe you were an endless giver or selfish yourself with a need to protect those around you. If she wasn't a good lover, maybe you turned her off or weren't interested in adjusting time schedules. Let's face it, it's easier to blame the other person for all the problems. But in marriages, it doesn't work that way. Problems are because of the relationship or lack of it and not necessarily because one of you is at fault.

2. <u>If you live in the past, you don't have to face the present</u>.
This is the person that always talks about how good it was, how wonderful the ex was as a spouse. It's like living up to a fantasy adventure for the new spouse and there is no way of competing. The new spouse always feels guilty because he or she doesn't provide as great a lifestyle as the spouse <u>used</u> to live. This living in the past can make life miserable for everyone involved. The reality of this situation is that even if the lifestyle was better (and many times it was not), there was a choice made to marry <u>you</u>. Living in the past prevents commitment for the present. It's an easy way out. For instance, Sally always reminded Tim of how her ex-husband fixed the cars. She forgot to mention that he did it to avoid spending time with her. Tim felt inadequate in the mechanical areas and even though he tried very hard, it was a useless endeavor. In retaliation, Tim started picking on Sally for the things she didn't do as well as his ex-wife. They were beginning a war and the battle seemed inevitable.

3. <u>Living in the past stops change for the future</u>.
In remarriage, many of us bring mementos of our past relationships. Paintings, pictures, furniture, and other objects serve to provoke memories. These items have some value, but often individuals use them to sadly reminisce how they managed to mess up their lives. Maybe our homes should be filled with

the present and our lives reflecting that attitude. The past can be reflected upon as a great teacher but not a constant reminder. For example, Bob and Susan couldn't sit in their furniture without past reminders. The kids chimed in and yelled about who owned "what" in the house. Even though they lost some money, Bob and Susan and the kids bought new furniture and lost some old memories.

4. <u>Settling the past makes us face insecurities</u>.

When you settle the past and have made amends with your conscience, you find yourself alone. This can be very scary. Maybe you can admit to what you've done with your life and how you have made mistakes. Facing up to ourselves is harder than dealing with anyone else. You are your strongest critic. If you find that you have lost relationships by your actions and ignorance, it is not so easy to forget. But looking at the dark parts of our past does help us escape its clutches. Facing our faults is the first step to change. Maybe you weren't around enough, too devoted to your job, were a constant criticizer, or couldn't communicate feelings. If you don't own that part of you, the same type of things will keep occurring in your present relationship. The scary part is that once you have faced yourself and admitted both your faults and attributes, you must move in to a second type of process involved in change. It's called action. Many of us talk about change forever and ever. Our words are great convincers of others but they do little to convince ourselves. The way that we really demonstrate that we are committed to change is by doing something different. This can have a great impact on the success of a relationship. "Maybe this time, I'll be around more and I'll listen to what my spouse says." That means setting time up each day to talk and spending less time working overtime. The action part of change is the hardest for all of us. Most of us like to make excuses of why life is so hard on us, but few of us resolve to make it different. That can be disastrous in a remarriage. The best stepfamilies have partners who admit that they are working hard to be the best that they can be even if that happens to be a lot of work. Changing in a relationship is hard but worth the effort. Jan agrees with this philosophy. "I was bringing into this new family stuff that everyone was giving me. My ex-husband, parents, and friends were not approving of my new marriage. Even after I got married, they were each giving me criticisms of my lifestyle and of my new husband. I was going crazy trying to please everyone. Finally, one day I realized that this was crazy. I knew what I wanted and if the people who were close to me didn't understand then too bad. The funny thing is that after I told all of them how I felt, they apologized and started accepting me as a person."

One of the ways of effecting change in the remarriage is to be open to discussing past marriages and their influence on how they affect the present relationship. It is worthwhile just to sit down and discuss the rights and wrongs of the past marriage with your new spouse. Questions you may want to talk about include these:

1. How was your courtship period?
2. What attracted you to your ex-spouse?
3. What was your marriage and honeymoon like?
4. How were the first years of your marriage?
5. What was it like having children (or not having any kids)?
6. What effects did the children have on the relationship?
7. How was your social life and friendships?
8. Did parents interfere in your marriage?
9. What were your sex roles in the marriage?
10. How was your sex life and sexual relations?
11. What events contributed to your feelings about the marriage?
12. What qualities are still the most likeable and dislikeable in your ex-spouse?
13. When you think about your ex-spouse, what do you think about?
14. How do you feel your children dealt with the divorce?
15. How do you feel about yourself and your past marriage?
16. What were the biggest mistakes you made in the marriage?
17. What is the most important thing you need now in a marriage?
18. What were the effects of career (spouse's and your's) on a marriage?
19. What is a perfect marriage to you?
20. How do you see yourself changing in the future?

It's amazing that some of us feel comfortable talking about everything _except_ our past relationships. You can discuss your childhood ad nauseum but it is difficult to discuss past lovers. It's like they must be kept secret. Sitting down and setting up a structured situation where each partner talks about the above-mentioned areas can be very helpful and enlightening for a spouse. It can take several hours or several days. Relating the material to your present lifestyle is important. Also, not using the discussion for "grudge or I'll get you" material is a must.

Some of these discussions disclose important material which can hinder a marriage. For instance, Nancy blamed her husband Stan for the demise of her marriage. Stan had been a good athlete and seemed to have a promising career in business. They had two children and everything seemed like a perfect American dream. As a teacher, Nancy became more and more interested in her career. She decided to pursue a Master's degree and was promoted to an administrative position. She and Stan saw less and less of each other as each person felt burdened by the children and their demands. Soon, all Stan and Nancy did was argue and fight. Stan saw Nancy as fighting a battle to defeat all males in order to have a successful career. Nancy saw Stan as egocentric and wanting a woman to cook and pick up after him.

Their divorce was a bitter affair with constant arguments ensuing over who should get certain material objects. Little consideration was given to the other person. This same situation continued after the divorce in the form of visitation arguments, income tax hassles, and numerous other items.

Nancy quickly met John to fill the gap in her life that was vacated by Stan. Their love affair was rapid and they soon married. At first, everything seemed fine. However, as the children settled in and the family had begun, Nancy noticed life was slipping away from her again. She was starting to have the same old problems but with a new face. "Are all men such chauvinists?" she asked. In their courtship, Nancy and John had forgotten to discuss the intimate details of running a house when both people work. Nancy assumed John would know her lifestyle and adapt himself accordingly. On the other hand, John felt likewise. Soon Nancy and John were each demanding their partner meet their expectations. Statements were bouncing all over the house, including "You don't help out enough, I expect a nice meal when I get home, I'm used to sex on Friday nights, we're eating too late, You're just a slob, just like ... ?"

When Nancy and John came into therapy, they were about to strangle each other. The anger they had for each other contained not only the present but also the past. In helping them sort out difficulties, both realized that it was unfair to carry all this "baggage" on their back into the relationship. We helped them put their secrets out in the open and they began to analyze why their past marriages failed. It is amazing to us how couples can also be very supportive of each other when they reveal their insecurities about themselves and their relationships. After a period of several months, Nancy and John were able to sort out what they wanted to bring into the relationship by their "choice" and not because it was habit. They also learned to develop new patterns and needs for their marriage and tried to share openly when either of them had a problem.

John and Nancy are not an unusual couple in the stepfamily. Situations can be quite explosive if they are not defused early. An example would be a couple that discusses some matters before marriage but changes the contract or their ideas soon after the marriage. Maybe they agree to be different than they'd been in their past marriage, but they have difficulty with the task. For instance, Joe used to nag his ex-wife about dressing nicer and looking sexier for him. After a while, he started nagging his new wife in the same way. Or Ally, who was insecure and dependent, became even more depressed and controlling than she had ever been with her new husband.

Breaking out of these old patterns can be very difficult. Usually they are learned in childhood and probably modeled from the same sex parent. That's why women with alcoholic fathers marry husbands who are alcoholic or become alcoholics. These women have learned from the same sex parent how to take care of an alcoholic. In 20 or 30 years, every day they witnessed this event. For this reason, these patterns become so ingrained in us that they become almost unrecognizable to us as individuals.

When you take a look at your first marriage, there were probably many factors that contributed to its demise. The most important factor was probably the relationship you had. Each person is a contributor to the success or failure of a marriage. Ignoring your past and defending one side (either good or bad) limits your effectiveness in the future.

Taking a look at your "family of origin," or original family, may also be very helpful. Trying to look at and understand your parents' relationship may give you some valuable clues as to how you perform in relationships. Many of us are caught in the bind of trying to find balanced sexual roles within a relationship. Much of what haunts both males and females are the sex roles they learned and observed from their parents. Even though American life has changed drastically in every aspect of our society since those times, you may still believe these roles to be the same in today's world.

Generally, old sex roles are proving to be ineffective. Economic factors, educational levels, childhood-rearing patterns, and cultural changes have impacted American life, and particularly the American family. Expecting sex roles to stay the same in a society that has advanced technologically and socially by leaps and bounds is almost ludicrous.

Marriage difficulties often emerge from the reality that few of us have experienced adequate sex roles from which to model. We are basically left with trying to develop new roles as we experience them.

Most couples are having trouble with this dilemma. Unfortunately, there are no simple answers to be offered. Although we will talk about this in a later chapter, the most important ingredient to success that we have found is a willingness to talk and negotiate about difficulties. The lost art of "compromise" is a more effective tool when trying to work on relationship problems. Breaking with the past and living in your present relationship is just as important. Dealing with messages or expectations from the past needs to be discussed openly between partners and understood by both people. Only after understanding can change occur.

For success in the stepfamily, the ex-spouse relationship must be put in proper perspective. The term "ex-spouse" means exactly what it says. You are no longer married and are no longer bound by that commitment. If you have children, you do what you feel is best for _them_ and not necessarily for the ex-spouse. If there is a cardinal rule, it is the following: "_Never_ choose your ex-spouse over your present spouse in _any_ circumstance. If you do, you will find yourself with a larger problem on your hands than when you started."

The Role of the Custodial Parent

The role of the custodial parent in the stepfamily is the most crucial and the most difficult. In most court cases in the United States, the woman or mother is awarded custody of the children. Even with our changing societal norms we believe this will be the rule and anything else "the exception," for many years to come. In all honesty, we will share our bias that we agree with the courts in most of these cases. This is usually based on some cultural factors inherent in our society that often prohibit the male from fully functioning as a single parent in an androgenous or equal relationship. In our opinion, women have a decided advantage. Because--

1. They are usually more affectionate to children and are able to understand and give the emotional support children need (particularly young children). Most men have trouble dealing with emotional issues with adults, let alone having to teach their own children. Carl Whittaker, a famous family therapist, summed it up succinctly when he said, "If I could have

three more sets of kids, maybe I could learn to love." It may be even more difficult for a man to love and care for children that are not his offspring. As a new father, to love your children may require more of a commitment and involvement than a parent normally does with the "natural child." Society makes it easy for the biological parent while the new parents' road is often uphill with sharp curves.

2. Women are trained in the essentials of daily caring for children. Most of them can cook, can talk to teachers, and can do many other chores men avoid like the plague. As former schoolteachers, we noticed how many conferences were loaded with Moms and no Dads. It's just not Dad's "place." Even male comedians joke about their inability to cope with changing sex roles. We heard one comic remark that he learned important things when he was young that helped him cope with life. These included playing baseball, kicking footballs, and watching Mom. Having a baseball bat doesn't help cook dinner!

3. Women are used to caring for children. They are often baby-sitters when they are growing up and are used to the developmental crises that occur in growing up. Usually they are the ones that watch brothers and sisters, even when they may not be the oldest.

We are not saying that males cannot learn to do these things well, but rather that most have to learn <u>how</u> to do them. They are not taught from birth like women, and this can be a distinct disadvantage for the male when he is in the courtroom when a judge is deciding who has the best attributes for being the custodial parent.

However, women are trained to be adequate "carers" of children and this may also create other problems. One of the major difficulties is that in the stepfamily a strong and assertive woman is required for survival. She will be the one who is being torn, divided, angry, depressed, protective, and experiencing numerous other emotional conflicts. She, and not the male, is the caretaker and stable unit within the family structure. Unfortunately, most women are ill-prepared for this battle and usually their happiness suffers because of it. The on-the-job training for this profession is unlike anything you have ever seen.

An analogy could be a boxer who keeps getting hit with blind side punches or ones he does not expect. If he would turn around and block the punches or fight back, he might have a chance of winning. Otherwise, he will be knocked silly until he finally loses. And nobody likes to lose, especially when it pertains to family. So it is with the custodial mother. Society and her family keep hitting her blindside with unrealistic expectations or "guilt trips" concerning how terrible life is for everybody. Many times, this Mom will feel like the burden of the world is on her shoulders and that there are no solutions. We believe that with a better understanding of her circumstances and the motives of the people around her, the custodial parent can be in a much better position to make decisions concerning herself and her family.

It is a disappointing idea to us that women are not taught to be assertive, and many have difficulties with the concept. There are few role models for them to choose from, whether in business or at home, where they can model good effective communication. Usually their mothers were lousy models in this area and were probably more manipulative than assertive. We believe that women are tired of being "cute" and sexually coy in order to get what they deserve from a male. Even if assertiveness can be a positive value for women, it usually is not reinforced by anyone. Certainly, men will not like it since it threatens them and takes away much of their power in a relationship. Other women don't like it because it makes <u>manipulation</u> by them more obvious and it shows that you are not one of the "gang." When you break the code, everyone gets angry. That's why E.R.A. is such an emotional issue.

In all reality, how could anyone not want another person to have an equal chance? But actions can be very different from words. In reality, assertiveness is just another catchy phrase that really means clear communication. And this is a process where all of us could increase our skills. However, as therapists we are not vain enough to think that some folks don't like clear talkers. This could be for many reasons, but people who can state their mind in a caring but straightforward manner usually require the same from the person with whom they are talking. Pretty soon this kind of conversation eliminates a lot of games between people and this can be both scary and healthy. The artful skill of talking can be very helpful to the stepfamily, both with spouses and children, or with friends and neighbors who generously share their negative opinions.

Marsha learned the art of communication the hard way. "When I got divorced, I was really confused. I went to my friends and instead of help all they gave me was hassle. Go back to your husband! You're leaving a good thing! Hell, I didn't need to hear that. All I wanted was somebody to listen to me. My parents weren't much help either. They acted like I was a terrible sinner and that I could ruin my kids' lives. All of this was too much for me and so I started talking to a therapist.

"After a while, I figured out that they were crazy and not me. Real friends wouldn't talk to me this way. So finally I started to stand up for myself and, you know, people started to treat me better. I guess they just didn't understand how I felt and what I was going through."

Sometimes what we think will keep us away from people actually draws us closer.

When we work with stepfamilies, we teach assertive communication skills to all family members, and particularly to Mom. Because she has always been a "carer and a giver," it's hard for her to stick up for her rights and not feel guilty. This guilt can ultimately be her downfall. She must learn to express her feelings to everyone involved, including children (from all marriages) and spouses (from all marriages). To help explain this, we tell a simple story. There was once a woman who had a friend who loved to talk. When she talked she stood close to her and stepped on her foot and stayed on it all the time she talked. In order not to offend the woman, because her conversation was enjoyable, this woman never told her friend about her habit of stepping on feet. Finally, one day, Greta, her best friend, got up the courage and said, "get off my foot." We believe that sometimes you have to tell people in your family to also get off your foot because it hurts. There is no justification for a person to treat you badly even (or especially) if this person is "family."

We would like to explore in detail the three main relationships where a woman needs to express her assertiveness and some typical examples of how people may "step on her feet."

1. <u>The Ex-Spouse and the Woman</u>

    After getting up the courage to fight for your rights in a divorce case, it's often hard to continue to battle. Everything is usually a hassle in a divorce, including settling property, dividing finances, negotiating child support, and agreeing upon visitation rights. Afterwards you feel like collapsing and not talking to this person like you used to "have to do." If only this were reality. Typically, communication with the spouse will be necessary, particularly in regard to the children. This communication can be quite manipulative and volatile for the custodial parent. Sometimes bitterness can get in the way of this communication.

    Dianne, an accountant with a major oil company, agreed. "I can talk to lots of influential people during the day but every time I hear Kevin's voice I cringe. He walked out on me and I still can't forgive him. I know it sounds mean but I try to get back at him as much as I can. If he wants to see the kids, then he can pay for it. I was so nice to him and all I got was a divorce in return. It seems like we can't talk about anything without getting into a fight. I'm tired of it."

    Another potential problem is the giver "aspect" of the woman. She often feels guilty that non- custodial Dad doesn't see the kids enough and this is reinforced by Dad as he moans about how life is terrible for him. This "life is terrible" routine may also be used for nonpayment of child support. If Dad is good at his sad routine, he usually can convince the kids to be on his side. Statements like "Oh, life is so lonely and desperate without you," or "I just sit all day long and think of you." This is often the father that Mom had to push into going out and doing something with the kids. Now, he has them for all the "fun and games." Being with Dad is like being at a carnival. No wonder the kids can't wait to see him. It is almost a perfect match for the child's egocentric behavior that believes in "getting all I can get."

"When Glenn would take the kids out for junk food and video games every weekend, I used to get very angry," relates Debbie. "Here I would be washing their clothes, making dinner, and getting them to school without a word of thanks. He drops in on the weekend and it's like Johnny Carson walked into their lives. It's all smiling faces. But then a friend in a similar situation talked to me and I think I understand better. I forget that he misses out on a lot of things, too. He's not there when the kids share about school, or if they have a big problem or when they need someone to care. Glenn was not very open with his emotions so I guess if he can't buy them things, there would be nothing left. To be honest, at times I feel sad for him. As the kids are getting older, they seem to be drawing towards George, their new dad, because he can talk to them. In fact the kids tell me Glenn keeps putting George down with abrasive comments so I know it must be bothering him that the kids like George."

Besides moaning about how lonely he is and getting the children on his side, the non-custodial parent may do whatever he pleases just to infuriate the custodial parent, which he usually does. It reminds us of an adolescent who is searching for freedom and wanting to retaliate at the same time. Parenting is thrown out the window by the ex-spouse and Mom ends up being the bad person who puts up all the restrictions. The non-custodial Dad will agree to whatever Mom says but will never do it. In fact, he will probably do the opposite.

An example of this is as follows: Joe, the ex-spouse, has no family of his own and so maintains contact with his ex-wife's parents in order to keep a sense of normality to the kids. So when the kids visit the grandparents, he just drops over for extra visitation time and grabs a meal or two. Grandma and Grandpa are placed in an awkward position and don't want to be total heels by asking him to leave. Instead, they invite him to supper. The kids think it's like old times and just giggle and laugh about how "nothing's" changed. Mom hits the roof, but realizes that she can't control her ex. She is forced to teach her parents the art of saying "no," or "we're busy," or "our daughter stated this is not your visitation time as you agreed." In an act of courage, Mom counts time spent with grandparents and children as visitation time for the next month. Soon after, the situation changes.

Even though this was a difficult situation, Mom was within her rights. She had arranged the time so that the kids could be close to their grandparents. She had mentioned to her ex that this would be a good time for them to be alone. When her ex-spouse deliberately used the situation for his own advantage, he ended up alienating his ex-wife and her parents. We believe that deliberate manipulation in this regard should have consequences and hence we agreed that using this time as visitation privilege was effective. Since the grandparents had not seen the ex-spouse in several months, it was anticipated that he would call before the next visit. Another reason this was important, too, was that the children needed to realize that the family situation had changed and that their new Dad was the person who had a relationship with Grandma and Grandpa, not the ex-spouse.

An effective rule for stepfamilies is that family unity comes first and not old family ties. The bond between the ex-spouse and children and <u>his</u> family was fine but not the ex-wife's family. In other words, he could share with his family as much as he wished.

Another hassle that may occur is if Dad tells the children that both Mom and the new Dad are "creeps." This can be quite upsetting. We believe that Mom needs to lend her perspective on the situation at this time. She should share with the children that she had good reasons to leave and that there is another side to the story. This isn't something to be done in a spiteful way, but it lets the children know you don't take any guff. If the custodial parent lets the little subtleties of the ex-spouse continue, she will be awaiting bigger trouble down the road.

It is also vital that the ex-spouse stay out of the stepfamily's house as much as possible. This means both physically, psychologically, and verbally. We've had clients who have had ex-spouses spend weekends with the kids in their houses, but this does not usually work. Also, talking about non-custodial Dad with the children should be kept to a minimum. His place is when they are with him and not with you. We point out to parents that the non-custodial parent doesn't spend much time talking about you, so why do you talk about him? We do realize that children do have concerns and these can be discussed. However, there is a difference between talking about concerns and constantly rattling about Dad and the past or how great Dad is. Sometimes kids don't want to admit that life can go on fine with a new parent and so they feel guilty and wish to relate to the past. Mom needs to point out that process and discuss it in the open. Your family discussions should focus on your family and not "his family." Live in the present and leave the past in the graveyard.

2. <u>The Kids and Mom</u>

The kids can make life in the stepfamily very difficult for the custodial parent and constantly try to stick her in the middle or place her in conflicting situations. The kids may not be willing to commit to their new family for many reasons and thus may choose to take out their anxieties on Mom.

As we have stated before, Mom must stick up for her new relationship with the new Dad no matter if the person does something right or wrong. If the kids sense that they can cause a split between the two of you, they often will be glad to provide the wedge. There is a simple test to find out if the kids are doing this. If you find that you are having a much better time as a couple when the kids are gone--you are not so desirous of having them back, then you have some troubles. Yes, everyone needs space <u>but</u> not space forged by children. Sometimes their actions can be quite subtle.

It took Julie a while before she realized what was happening in her case. "The kids seemed to be always talking about the past and arranging problems so that either they or I had to call my ex-spouse almost daily. After a while, I found that I was neglecting Todd and that the kids were also avoiding him. So I started to pull out and kept spending more time with Todd. Boy, did the kids get angry! Even my ex-husband tried to get me in the act by saying that he needed to talk to me each day about the kids. Well, I stuck to my guns and in a crazy way the kids respected it. I told them they could live in the past all they wanted, but I was in love with Todd and that they were missing a good thing. Finally, they came along and now life is a lot easier."

We believe it is important that Mom defend the new Dad in front of the children and support him. Arguments can be discussed later in private. This is particularly important in the beginning of the relationship. She must also push the children to spend time with him. Think up activities to do together and ones they can do alone with him. Mom must work hard at developing a relationship between the children and new Dad. It is not going to happen if you just "wish it." It takes work and planning.

If the kids are always saying negative things about the new parent, state positive attributes or ignore this. When the children misbehave out of anger or not wanting to conform to new family rules, they must be disciplined. Otherwise, your house will be in chaos. We always warn new families that the children will test you. It is a child's way.

As we have stated before, when your spouse's children come to visit, they must also be treated with respect and love. Teach all the children to obey the rules of your house and do not change for temporary visitors. Show the children methods of getting along and if they vie for special attention, ignore it. The father will want to treat the visiting children differently, but he can't. If he does, only trouble will result. Messages like "they're special," "they get extra privileges," "he loves them more than us," can be disastrous truths for the stepfamily. The way to stop this is to not put yourself in the situation. Everyone must be treated the same no matter the special circumstances.

As a final note in regard to the children, we stress that love, caring, and discipline can break down any walls, no matter how high. Consistency will be your key to success.

3. The New Dad and the Kids

The most difficult act for the woman is being stuck between her new husband and the children. This can be disastrous for all involved. As we've stated before, the wife owes primary allegiance to the husband. However, the husband owes some strong commitment also.

Let's take a look at some problems that males can have with the stepfamily. They're usually three discrepancies:

   a. Marrying a male that doesn't want children. If this is true, then tell him to find someone else. Marrying this person will drive everyone bananas and it's an ultimate cop-out. When you marry in the stepfamily, you marry the kids, too. This male would be better off marrying a woman without kids. He will be miserable and so will the kids and you. This is just like the person who is in a job for the money and hates the work. Eventually this person quits or goes crazy.

   b. The male who refuses to be a parent. This is another typical male cop-out. They're your kids so you raise them. The response is "They're our kids and we raise them." The male may often run away from commitments and good parenting means giving love to a child. Before getting married, each spouse must be willing to work at loving the children and believing that they are their own children. The male must get involved and be with the children both alone and with you. Structured time is a must and Mom often has to force this arrangement. Commitment in a relationship in a stepfamily means getting everyone involved. Nobody gets off easy.

c. <u>My kids are different</u>. The male cannot treat his biological kids better than the other children. This will only cause resentment and hassles. All parties must be treated as equally as possible. No excuses are accepted. This point should be discussed and cleared from the beginning. The kids should not have a decision in this matter as to how things should be structured. They can have some input but the decision is made by the parents. They set up the standards and the kids live within them.

In looking at the custodial parents' role in blending, we concede that it is very difficult. Since it is almost always the woman, she has to learn to be assertive and to structure a family so that all get involved. At times, she may feel like giving up, but she can't! She may want to be left totally alone, but she can't!

Everyone must have his or her say and share input, but Mom will generally be the strategist that helps it work. If she does well (and gets some help), the family will prosper. We have seen it happen over and over again.

Dilemmas of the Step Parent

Unlike the dilemma of the custodial parent, the new parent faces a different situation.

Usually the full-time new parent is a male because the custodial parent is often female and therefore it entails some unique characteristics. Women face this dilemma often on a part-time basis with kids visiting weekends, summers, or even daily. However, women who are full-time new parents are increasing.

No matter what sex, for this person it is a "damned if I do, damned if I don't" situation. As a male, he may end up paying for two families with kids in both and not gaining the respect of either household. As a female, it seems like she is trying to unite two different families.

John would be a typical example of the trapped father. Having been married for 15 years, his divorce settlement put him in financial trouble. Paying large child support payments, he saw his two boys Wednesday nights and Sundays.

Two years after his divorce, he remarried Sally who had a young son. John grew to love this boy like his own sons. A year later he and Sally had another child, a little girl.

All these children and families cost John dearly. After several years, he was over $18,000 in debt, but this was only part of the problem. It seemed like nobody cared a damn about him and his life. His ex-spouse would constantly call him and berate him for not being an adequate father. "I can't do it alone," she lamented as tears ran down her telephone. She would demand items that were not in their legal agreement and tell the children their father was cheap and was ruining their lives.

If he spent money on them, he would hear complaints from his new wife. "All your money goes to her and those kids. What about us?" she would yell. When his sons came to visit, it was a disaster. They treated Sally and everyone very harshly, almost all of it to gain revenge for not having the family they wanted. The fights were unbearable as everyone seemed to get into the act. Because of the chaos, John and Sally were at each other's throats constantly.

The answer to John's problem is not very simple. He cannot control his ex-spouse, but it appears he needed support from his present wife. In therapy, Sally's leadership and involvement were increased with significant results appearing because of this. John and Sally were taught how to communicate their side of the story to each other and each person became more open-minded. This led the way for behavior change. Sometimes the stepfamily places us in situations in which we feel uncomfortable or do not wish to be. Avoiding these areas just aggravates situations. It's like a cold that we never seem to take care of and so it never seems to go away. Problems need to be faced and solved (preferably when they're small). The hardest part may be figuring out the solution to the problem.

We admit that in many instances the male is placed in a very difficult situation. However, it is impossible to control one's ex-spouse and tell her how to raise the kids or explain proper ways to spend child support. It is a useless activity to yell, scream, argue, fight, and moan. However, we do believe that the male needs to break his bonds with the ex-spouse which strongly tie him into their relationship. Yes, it is important that he stay in close contact with his children. But we have seen many ex-spouses who still act as if they are married. In other words, the male is emotionally committed to two women. In other countries they call this bigamy, but in America it's called the stepfamily.

We have worked with couples where the male will deny this vehemently. His words may sound fine, but his actions are quite different. He is talking to her on the phone every day, gives her money, shares intimate secrets, and even fixes things around the house. Occasionally, they may even experience sexual intercourse.

Whether it is due to our culture or not, most marriages cannot withstand this type of pressure or strain. In reality, it is like the male having an acceptable mistress where the wife is not allowed to disagree.

It is not that we are saying that the male cannot have some type of relationship with the ex-spouse, but there must be an emotional line that is drawn and is also suitable to the new spouse. On the average, our belief is that the more the ex-spouse is kept out of the stepfamily, the better the family will function.

We do believe the legal agreement should be honored by the male but that extra benefits should be agreed upon by the new spouse. Sometimes the strain of trying to be a good father and providing everyone with everything can be too much. It is unrealistic to assume that this can be done with the financial difficulties that most couples are experiencing. Somewhere in the process, someone is going to be deprived. In most cases, it should be the ex-spouse even if she/he decides to "take it out" on the kids. For the male placed in this situation, it is best that he give his love to his children when he is with them and get on with life. Otherwise, he will grow to become a bitter person who is bounced like a "yo-yo" between two families.

For the female new parent, the conflicts may be different, but the emotional intensity is just as involved. Since women are often better in "caring" positions than males, the emotional dilemmas involved in being a new Mom can be very difficult. New Moms are notoriously seen as evil persons because they are the ones who set the character and structure of the family and may be around more than the male even if both people are working. Having to hold this position of emotional responsibility and bonding can be a great burden for the female. The children may be reluctant to attach because they may believe they are becoming a traitor to their natural parent or they may realize the emotional bond the new Mom represents. New mothers often set the family rules and guidelines for behavior and hence are viewed as "deprivors" rather than carers.

In these circumstances, we believe the new Mom should proceed slowly, but that she should not jeopardize her beliefs about how a family should be. The father must also be very supportive, for the children will quickly play one parent against the other. Parents must realize that they are often viewed as "mean" when they say no, and this may be even more true with the new parent. It is when the new Mom continually gives in to be liked, or when the father is drawn to the side of the children, that major hassles will start.

Another dilemma for the new parent is moving from the role of friend to parent in both the eyes of the child and the spouse. Each person will have trouble with this new instant identity. Processes like these take time but it <u>must</u> be time effectively used.

Jack found the role change from friend to parent to be difficult. "The kids talked to me about everything before Lillie and I got married. Afterwards, it took a while for them to accept me again. I had to set down rules just like Lillie so I wasn't the good guy all the time. But after a few months they grew to understand me and care for me deeper than they had before. I guess it was worth all the aggravation."

There are several ways we would like to share which can be helpful in orienting to this type of change:

1. Discuss the changing relationship from friend to parent with each other before the marriage. What ramifications will this have within the family? Be direct on how you expect the children to act, not necessarily how they feel like acting. Respect is a key requirement in this process. The child's words must be listened to but respect for the new parent is <u>expected</u>. This means courtesy, involvement, caring, and a reasonable effort. Not only is this required of the child, but also the parent. As we have previously discussed, the custodial parent can often help float or sink this relationship in a hurry.

If you are being misused, speak up. "At first, I couldn't believe this was happening to me," shared Leslie, a new mother of three children. "The kids would say snotty things and John would stand by not wanting to get involved. He was afraid to hurt them and was so guilty that he had broken up a perfect home. Even if I was nice, the kids still were mean to me. They refused to do tasks and contributed nothing. Finally, I got so mad one day that I told them they could all pack their bags and live somewhere else. I also told John to start standing with me or he'd be standing alone. Funny thing, they finally got the message."

2. The parents also need to discuss with the children the new relationship that will develop before the marriage, particularly in regard to parenting roles. The involvement of each parent and "their children" must be understood explicitly. Agreements can be reached and problems avoided. Preventative medicine is always the best cure. This does not mean that the children have the final say as to what will occur in the house. Rather, we mean that everyone has input into a newly developing lifestyle and that surprises are reduced to a minimum. Every person has expectations of how living in a house should be. Sometimes, these expectations are more understood if they are shared rather than kept secret.

3. Each spouse needs to be committed to the other spouse's children. When you marry in a stepfamily, you marry the children, too! If not, you are usually doomed. We are not

talking about instant love. What we are saying is that children deserve caring and involvement from an adult. This means involvement that you would want as a child and that's usually plenty. If you are not committed to the concept of family, then don't be surprised to find that you don't have one. Is this hard? You bet it is. But what isn't that's worth anything in life? Hard work and effort are ingredients to success. And if there is one major problem to stepfamilies, this may be it. If you do not care or spend time with your spouse's children right from the beginning, the relationship will be always struggling! It forces the parent to be stuck between the children and the spouse with each vying for attention and complaining about the other. We also see the adult as the person who begins the relationship and who persists even when they are hassled.

4. We believe part-time children deserve full-time commitment. Often the new parent in this situation will beg not to be involved. "They're just awful to me." However true this is, the spouse deserves some respect for his or her children. An honest effort must be made and this doesn't mean just one-time shots. Don't exclude yourself from your spouse and children. Force yourself to be a part. Become involved in all of your spouse's life. Don't miss out on such important parts of his or her life even if it seems easier at first.

When Jim and Julie came for therapy, Julie disagreed with this assumption. Even though Jim tried very hard to love her children, Julie rejected his. "They're like teenage vultures. They come in and walk straight to the refrigerator. When I try to talk to them, they say you're not my mother. They are also rude to my kids and I don't see why I have to take that abuse. If they want to see Jim, let them meet at a movie theater or, better yet, a supermarket."

Little known to Jim and Julie, the kids were playing the perfect game. They had stuck themselves between the two of them and were effectively breaking up the marriage. Both Jim and Julie had a point, but the emotions involved in the issue could not let them resolve it. Although the solution involved some complex behavior, the premise was fairly simple. When the kids came to visit, Jim had to set some expectations of appropriate behavior or they could not visit. On the other hand, Julie had to engage in behaviors and activities that showed she cared for the children even if they rejected her.

We believe the "your" versus "our" mentality is often the downfall of the stepfamily. If spouses split the stepfamily into separate entities, then everything becomes confused. The roles in a family are so intertwined that if one person pulls out or refuses to accept the responsibilities of a parent, a child, or a spouse role, then chaos occurs. Family life has developed over centuries because it is a survival force. It can be the shelter and also the love reservoir from which we need to gain our sanity. If the family becomes confused, so do the family members.

The new parent role can be very confusing and the problems for the male and female step-parent are usually different. Their roles are more often culturally or "court-room" defined. The male is normally the person who moves into the stepfamily and assumes "new children" on a full-time basis. This is a difficult role even with a spouse who is 110 percent supportive of the new husband. Many of the battles are internal for the male.

Like the lion who dominates the litter of cubs, the male must feel he is in control and is needed. Sometimes when the very young are handled by others, animals will discard them because of their foreign smell. A likewise analogy can be made for the male. Many messages will float through his head that push him toward withdrawal.

1. These kids were raised by some other guy.
2. They walk, talk, and eat like him.
3. They do everything opposite of me.
4. Nobody ever says they look like me.
5. I'm living in a house of foreigners.
6. They don't ever give me proper respect a la Rodney Dangerfield.
7. When will they ever start doing things the right way ... my way.
8. It's a hopeless battle, he tells them to do things one way and I tell them another.

Besides these statements of doubt, the male is also used to a previous way of life. He, too, must adapt to a new family, and at first he may not jump at the experience. This is a time of grave doubt as the male wonders if this was the right decision.

Leo Roster says that many of us never get to be adults, we just grow up to be big children. The stepfamily needs a male adult, a person that is willing to sacrifice for long-distance payoffs or benefits. A male who can give love and expect little in return. Children will have difficulty adjusting to the concept of a new parent, particularly in the beginning. Many of us want to be instant successes and assure that in a few weeks we will have things straightened out. This is dead wrong in most cases.

The stepfamily takes time. If a family has been in a pattern for five, ten, or fifteen years, it takes a good year or two of hard work to make lasting changes. The male must understand that he must be a leader but to expect defeat along the way. When he loses, he still must go on. Each victory, no matter how small, should be cherished. Most of all, the parent must spend time with the children. This is particularly important when the kids or you do <u>not</u> want to be together. The adult must structure the time needed for development of relationships even if the children are reluctant. It goes along with the axiom that the more you see a face, the more you grow to like it. So show your face!

The male can have tremendous impact on the child if he is willing. He must learn to believe that these are his children and should treat them accordingly. One of the greatest joys for the male is seeing a child that starts to act like himself. It's true that imitation is the highest form of flattery.

Societal messages may also be a hamper. The non- biological parent is reminded by others that these are not "his children," but yet will ostracize him if he is remiss in his duties. Often the children will not have his name, which we believe is damaging to the parent, the child, and the entire family. The child will have to constantly explain his different name and be forced to introduce this parent in an awkward way. For example, Tim is closer to his non- biological father than to his other Dad and so when he introduces his "closer" parent he gets confused. "This is my father, well my new father, oh you know what I mean."

Yes, *we* know what you mean, Tim. It means that you can't demonstrate how you feel without a societal put-down, "New Dad."

We believe this can be a sore point for many families. The biological parent stands fast to his guns and will not let the child use a different name because he will lose his genetic offspring. In our work, we have found that this pride can often hurt the child and make life more difficult than necessary. In many cases, it would be nice if the child had a dual identity, particularly if the parents are geographically distanced. The child could use the last name of the parent that he was with at the time. If he was with the non-custodial parent, then he could use his name. Likewise, the situation would be the same with the "new name" of the custodial parent. This could be most effective for small children who develop strong attachments to both the biological and non-biological parent. When the child reaches age, he or she could decide on a last name. At the present time, some schools do this and work with parents if they are asked; however, as you are aware, legal complications "could occur" if one parent wishes to push a point or wants to seek revenge. It is sad when this occurs because we have seen the "portable" last name work for many children when parents are distant.

The female non-biological parent usually has a different role. Sometimes, it's part-time or weekend parent. It's hard to be a parent when you only have someone for a little while.

The children are so often entertained by the father that no one sits still for 15 minutes. Many males have trouble talking to their children and so instead drag them through shopping malls, movies, dinners, football games, and anywhere you don't have to converse. This puts Mom as the person who tags along, or, more than likely, sits at home.

Real-life relationships are created by everyday experiences and this "circus" can end up being quite a hassle. If Mom is to be a part of this weekend family, then she should have a "normal" part. If not, tell Mom to take weekend vacations. Instead, she is too often stuck in the middle and is neither parent nor friend. No benefits but lots of dirty work.

We believe weekend Moms can have a relationship if they try. This can be done in several ways:

1. Make some rules that apply for the family <u>all</u> the time and stick to them. What they do in another house is someone else's business.
2. Give the weekend kids a space to live. Make them feel a part of the family.
3. Give them some chores to help out around the house and yard. Work can also give you a feeling of belonging.

4. All vacations lead to resentment by other family members and may cause "favorites" who don't appreciate their special status.

5. Call the kids once in a while and you say hello. Talking helps you get closer (at least that's what all those commercials tell us).

In this part-time situation, the spouse can be a valuable support system. She must help you become a part by being positive towards your actions rather than being critical (and supporting your daughter or son). Comparisons to past-parenting lead to unnecessary quarrels and complications. If the children visit regularly or even every day, the new Mom's role is even more important. If she can create an atmosphere of acceptance, we have seen children fit in rather easily. The most important value that we see as integral to this process is that children feel they are important and that they belong. If the parent understands a child's egocentric needs, the battle will be easier.

The new parents, whether male or female, need to realize that failure is a part of the process of unity. If you learn by your mistakes and leave a path for change, your chances for success are greater. Success means a functional family that provides emotional, psychological, and physical support for all family members. At times, parents, children, and friends will give you little confidence. Pats on the back may be few in number. Your gratification will come in developing strong and loving relationships over a period of time. We have no timetables to give. Sometimes it takes months, for others it may be years. As a general rule, it takes at least one or two years to develop a strong family. It is up to you to begin the process and to determine your success.

Preventing Friction in the Stepfamily

There comes a point in almost any relationship when people wonder whether they belong in the relationship or why they got into this mess in the first place. The stepfamily may be even more trouble than what you bargained for when you decided to marry.

Some people will say that once you've been divorced, it gets easier the next time. Hence, this may be one of the reasons people get married three, four, or five times. We do not necessarily agree with this assumption. We believe divorce is a painful process, one most of us do not want to repeat. People may get divorced several times because they repeat their same lifestyle and problems over and over again. It is not that they like divorce, it's just that they keep on living miserable lives.

We remember one couple that had to get divorced in order to get close to each other again. They had a type of love-hate relationship. When it was going good for them, it seemed like heaven. However, when it was bad, you could imagine the fury between them. The main focus of their relationship was that they couldn't live with each other and couldn't make it without the other person either. So they would go along until they reached a pretty severe crisis and they would divorce. A couple of months after the divorce they could start dating again and soon thereafter they would remarry. This procedure went on for three or four times as their lives alternated between happiness and misery.

In working with couples, we have found many people who have said that if they worked as hard the first time as they did in their second marriage, they probably never would have been divorced the first time. So we think that many folks give a sincere effort to trying to make their marriage and their stepfamily work.

On the other hand, keeping the romance going after you have been in a stepfamily for a period of time can be trying. After you've passed the honeymoon stage and start learning what your spouse is really like, you start to have second guesses. We believe marriages fail in stepfamilies for many reasons, but we would like to discuss a few which we think are the most common.

1. <u>There is a lack of support system within the relationship.</u>

If either partner feels that a spouse is not 100 percent supportive, then trouble may be brewing. In a world where many people feel they aren't important and suffer from the consequences of technology and huge conglomerates, it is vitally important that someone believes in you. You need to feel secure and to know that your dreams can <u>maybe</u> become realities. If a spouse is constantly putting you down, arguing, and fighting about silly inconsequential matters, and pitting you against the children, then life is a tougher road to travel. In the end, some people choose aloneness rather than swallow this bitter pill.

As a business executive, Phil made countless decisions affecting the lives of many people. However, in his family Phil was in constant trouble. He disagreed with Pat on how to raise the kids and seemed to have little power as a new father. Each time he would ask the children to do something, they would either refuse to do it or see their mother in order to avoid the work. He and Pat constantly were in argument and their relationship began to dwindle. Phil became more bored with his wife's conversation because it lacked the stimulation of his business encounters. Pat interpreted his unattentive behavior as unloving and she put more of her time into the children's activities. As time went on, each of them spent more and more time apart (he at work and she with the kids). It was no surprise, Phil eventually decided to leave.

2. Household sex roles are confused and misunderstood.

This is when each partner expects the other to do the work. Neither will give in or compromise because he or she will lose either "liberty or machismo." What occurs is that every single chore becomes a focal point for a huge argument, or a task is done but with great resentment. Often these couples will have unrealistic expectations, before they get into a marriage, that are based on the past spouse's inadequate treatment. A couple would be better off hiring a maid than to try to work out the emotional trauma of their difficulties. They fight over each meal, the dishes, the vacuum cleaner, ad nauseum. It appears that both keep a tally sheet of what they do and what the other person does not accomplish. Criticism is the typical mode of conversation as each person tells the other his or her inadequacies. Nobody does a task without a "woe is me" conversation. Living in this household can be a living torment.

3. <u>The children are the main focus of the marriage.</u>

If you find your whole life revolving around the children, wondering where they must be, what activities they must be involved in, and planning every weekend around their needs, then some problems may be occurring. When a couple and their needs are secondary to their children, it may indicate that the couple has lost common adult interests. It is true that children are very demanding, but they should never overrule the couple's need for common adult activities that will last long after the kids are gone.

Bill and Sherry are an example of a couple we believe fits this description. Married for 22 years, they had raised their two sons and a daughter quite admirably. The youngest was finishing high school and the other two were in college. For years Sherry had driven the kids to all their activities and also helped work in a grocery store that she and Bill owned. Bill had also participated in activities with the boys, particularly in later years. This was rewarding for him and somewhat different since he had traveled extensively when the kids were young and left much of the caretaking to Sherry.

Though they had spent increased time with their children, it appeared that Bill and Sherry had grown distant over the years. Recently, they sold the grocery store and Sherry was starting a new career at a local bank. Bill had reached a managerial position in a small company, but his opportunity for further advancement was very limited. With their daughter leaving for college in several months, both Sherry and Bill wondered what was left for them. They seemed to have little in common and the activities they each liked were vastly different. In recent months, Bill had been seeing another woman in her mid-30's who Bill stated was "more alive." Not surprisingly, Bill and Sherry decided to separate to determine their feelings for each other.

4. Sexual activities are infrequent or judged to be inadequate by at least one spouse.

We believe that everyone has a sex drive and that it is a basic biological mechanism for survival. Problems that exist in the relationship usually show up in the bedroom. When the sexual relationship is lacking, so too is the caring of the couple. Sexual sharing is an intense way of loving someone and helps people become close.

Sexual problems that we see are numerous. Some common examples are

- a wife who submits once weekly because she "has to" and abhors the experience
- the male who has numerous extramarital affairs but can't touch his wife

- the man who talks the great romantic life to friends but is only "self-satisfying" in bed with his wife
- the woman who still acts like a teenage virgin and is unwilling to experiment because it is sinful. The "missionary position" is hard enough
- the man or woman that demands a physically fit partner but can hardly fit on the bed
- the male or female who is constantly harassing the partner to look like a T.V. model
- the male that forces his wife to have sex whether she likes it or not
- the spouse that doesn't want to interrupt T.V. because it's "a good show"
- the spouse that reads a magazine article and believes they are not having enough sex to meet national standards
- the female that refuses to understand her body or is so ashamed that the room is as dark as a mine shaft
- the partner that demands orgasm as soon as you get into bed
- the male that can never express feelings or can only say "I love you" after he's had intercourse.

A sexual problem means a relationship problem. It affects all aspects of the marriage. Trying to hide it doesn't work nor does avoiding it. The only way to solve it is to admit the problem and then to face it. If you can't solve it, seek competent help.

Sometimes seeking help can be a difficult chore. For example, Carla came to counseling with both a relationship and a sexual problem. "Hal and I have been experiencing difficulties for over 10 years in our marriage," she shared. "He's a premature ejaculator and sex is very unsatisfying for me. Besides that, we argue most of the time. It seems like we have sex as if we are on a clock. Certain days of the week and specific times are designated and we can't seem to get out of the pattern. I can just tell by the way he acts that I'm supposed to give in. Well, lately I haven't been so willing. I've asked him to go to a specialist but he won't do it. He went to our family doctor about seven years ago and he was told he had a mild case of diabetes. The doctor said this could affect his sex life. Well, that was all he needed. He said he couldn't do anything about it and that was that. To tell you the truth, I just don't see it that way. I have set up appointments for him to see a specialist or a urologist and he seems to avoid going by creating all sorts of excuses. Finally, I read that therapists could help with some sexual difficulties so I made an appointment but he still refuses to go and talk about it. He says it's my problem. I guess he's right. My problem is him."

5. <u>The romance is disappearing and each day is the same experience.</u>

To keep a relationship alive, romance must be an integral part. Too many folks begin to take a spouse for granted, hence the relationship starts to dwindle. You need to take unexpected vacations, give unannounced affection and presents, laugh about your insecurities, etc. Romance is excitement and all of us could use a little more thrill in our lives. A lack of romance can mean that the caring is also dwindling.

Besides these points, it's important to remember that spouses in stepfamilies are normally trying for a second time. This usually leaves you with images of a first spouse and that past life or memories to contend with and to come to terms with.

Even though your first spouse may have left you desperately sad and confused, it wouldn't surprise us if you picked a new spouse with the same traits that distressed you in your first marriage. If so, you'll get in the same types of struggles and problems that you supposedly had left behind. These arguments and disagreements are harder to take the second time around and your patience may be limited. It helps to realize that if the same problems are occurring over and over again, then you must share part of the blame.

Mike's first wife was the controlling, nagging, type of person that you would leave rather than talk to or discuss a problem with. His new wife was very non-controlling until about six months into the marriage. The process was gradual, but Mike never noticed. She started calling him if he was five minutes late from work and she was always afraid he was with another woman. It was beginning to be a tough bind for everyone because most of the real messages were not being communicated. His wife was afraid he would leave because he had done this once already ... he had left with her. This time he might leave without her. So why not be afraid? Mike added to this dilemma by talking about how nice other women looked and acted as if his present wife wasn't up to standard.

She never could satisfy him, no matter what she did, so her only recourse left was to "make sure" he never had a chance to see anybody.

Mike couldn't see this and so he pushed for more freedom, as she sought control. They had forced a power battle from where there was no escape. In a small fashion, Mike also rejected the control because he felt he was being smothered. He was getting too much affection and feelings of insecurity from his spouse because she was afraid.

As the problem compounded, Mike started rejecting all parts of his wife and was on the road to another divorce.

It's obvious that recognition of your past patterns can help you deal with them in the future. For Mike and his spouse, new behaviors were in order for each person. We believe for a relationship to last, both partners must work at it.

A scary part for Mike and other folks is that you may want to bail out of the marriage before it hurts too much. Many people stay in marriages the first time that they should have left years ago. However, this causes a repercussion in second marriages. Rather than dealing with hurt, you may want to run from it. You expect the depth of a 10-year relationship in six months. This just may not happen. Part of the growth of any relationship comes through sticking through the hard times and making a "go" of it. If you are finding the problems in your second marriage are like your first, then it might be good to take a good long look at yourself rather than at your spouse. You may have more of a part in your troubles than you wish to admit. It's easier to blame your problems on others, jobs, bosses, kids, etc. However, it's hard to change another person (it's virtually impossible) and much easier to change your own ways.

Sometimes you may forget that your spouse may just be reacting in the best way that he or she knows how. Unless you learn alternative behaviors for you and your spouse, it can be a useless game. Introspection into the past can be a help. Besides your old spouses, you often bring your brothers, sisters, and parents into a relationship. After all, your parents were the ones that taught you "how to" have a marriage, "how to" love, and "how to" parent. If they were poor parents or inadequate role models, then you could have some problems. It requires some extra struggling to overcome past family messages if you don't realize or confront the issues. Besides having some time for personal introspection, it may be worthwhile to sit down and talk with your spouse about your family and messages they taught you. Some of the things you may want to talk about include:

1. Describe your relatives. Were any a bit odd or crazy?
2. How was love shown in your family?
3. Describe your relationships with brothers and sisters.
4. What was your first memory as a child?
5. Describe your mother, your father.
6. Describe the men in your family, and then the women or vice versa.
7. Who was the boss in the family?
8. How did each of your parents deal with your ex- spouses' personality traits?
9. Who was the stronger parent?
10. How were conflicts resolved by parents?
11. What were the major areas of disagreement among your parents?

One important point to consider is that even if your parents' marriage was successful, it was composed of persons from past generations. Their techniques of success may not work so well in our present marriage situations. The types of conflicts that modern couples face are very different from those faced by couples in the past.

If there are any ingredients important in keeping a marriage together, they are faith in each other, compromise, and communication. By faith, we mean the belief that both persons are acceptable as they are and that each person changes at his or her own pace. Just because you want someone to be a certain way doesn't mean this will happen. Too often people go into a relationship believing that they will mold their spouse into what they want. This sounds ludicrous but it happens. They can be sloppy or not help around the house before a marriage and it is "cute." After a marriage, it can start a volcanic eruption. If you accept people as they are, you have a better chance of success.

When we talk about compromise, we're not advocating pushing the person into what you had in mind. Rather, it means discussion and the willingness to give up some things for the benefit of the marriage. Certainly we don't mean compromising your integrity, but neither do we mean being a stubborn ox. Marriage is a give-and-take situation and the more you give to the relationship, the more you'll get in return.

Last but not least is communication. This is sitting down and discussing both problems and happy moments in a relatively easy tone. Arguments lead to nowhere and accomplish virtually nothing, in our opinion, except hurt feelings. Communication is the vital core of a relationship. If you don't let people in your lives and your world, you can't expect them to understand you. We believe that it's good to communicate what happens in our daily lives no matter how mundane it is. Setting time aside each day for discussion, sharing, and communication adds excitement to a marriage. Otherwise, we may find the loved person just slipping away, which can be disastrous. Without daily contact, we may lose focus, and communication and caring is something that all of us need.

Creating a Family Atmosphere

Disciplining children and creating a family atmosphere is a difficult task in any situation. The stepfamily is no exception to this rule.

In our culture, the parent provides a very important role in the security of a child. Children are very dependent on their parents for self-concept and love. If a marriage has ended, the children may have trouble getting close again. This creates a gap in stepfamily relationships where these relationships can become less harmonious and feelings may be uncertain.

In looking at the stepfamily, there may be some common problems which make it difficult for effective parenting to occur. These problems occur in the natural family, too, but they seem even more crucial to a remarried couple. Usually, in a couple, one parent is stricter than the other. However, over a period of time, a system of discipline begins to evolve and each partner begins to accept the other's opinion. With the stepfamily, the newer partner or parent may be a threat not easily dismissed. For example, a non-biological father attempts to discipline children with whom he has a much briefer relationship than the custodial parent. His style could be unfamiliar both to the children and to the mother. Serious arguments may then occur. Mom wants help with discipline and yet she wants to control the amount and manner. Even though she needs relief from the responsibility, she feels protective and doesn't want interference in the raising of her children.

Battles like this can be avoided before causing hurt and conflict. It's important to consider that stepfamily parents do not have the luxury of evolving a parenting style but have to plunge into the relationship. Besides beginning a new marriage, you have to determine the family structure and rules. That's not an easy task!

Juan and Mary were a typical couple that could never decide on a style of discipline. Each of them seemed to be on opposite sides of every issue. Juan would have high expectations for the children and he believed that hard work was the only sure way to achieve success. Mary thought that life was full of happiness and that you should try to avoid work as much as possible and seek exciting things to do. The children always seemed caught in the middle. The messages they received from each parent confused them and usually they ended up doing what they wanted but didn't feel very good about their decisions.

If one of the kids wanted to do something, it was easy to play one parent against the other. Eventually, Juan and Mary fought so much that they decided their marriage wasn't worth the hassle.

Discipline also involves love, and this can be an area of conflict for the remarried couple. Many times one parent will feel guilty about a past relationship and leaving children behind. This will make it difficult to get close to the new children. Warmth and love may be hard to show to new children because of the hidden anger of possibly being denied the right to see the children from a previous marriage and to give them the same amount of time and consideration. The new children may also have trouble dealing with their anger, and instead of expressing it towards the biological parent, they may direct it at the new parent because this person is an easier target. Discussing and getting these feelings out in an open, constructive manner can be helpful.

When Charlotte came for counseling, she believed it was all her fault. No matter how hard she tried, the kids never liked her. In trying to understand the problem, we noticed that there were some difficulties that were not due to Charlotte's arrival.

Several years before the remarriage, the children's original mother had left because she could not stand the strain of the marriage. Because of economic pressures, she had left the children with their father. Recently, she had moved back to the area and sought to re-establish herself with the kids.

The children had felt confused and angry by their mother's actions. However, they didn't want to antagonize for fear that she would go away again. Instead, they blamed all their problems on Charlotte and she received the brunt of their anger. In order to feel okay about themselves, the kids had made their mother more perfect than she was and picked on every fault of Charlotte's they could find. It wasn't until these issues were brought up at a family meeting that Charlotte realized what was actually happening to her. Understanding the circumstances allowed Charlotte to point out the unfairness of the situation and enabled her husband to stand by her when facts were distorted.

We believe discipline is a key to family success. This is not harsh abuse or physical punishment but rather it is establishing consequences for a child's misbehavior. Alfred Adler, a famous psychologist, stated a very important principle when he said, "discipline is the seed from which freedom grows."

An example may help in understanding this principle. Suppose you had a large group who just came to a beautiful resort. They were all lying around a pool and the hotel manager came out to meet everyone. She stated that you can do almost anything that you want at the resort, including swimming, fishing, tennis, badminton, golf, sailing, and many other things. After her talk, all went their separate excited ways. All except for Johnny, who was sitting by the side of the pool. He never learned how to do anything other than swim, so he could do nothing else during his vacation. He had not acquired the discipline which helped him to be free. Contrary to popular belief, his lack of discipline had limited his freedom to choose.

So too, we do this with children and families. Sometimes, all the members in a family are allowed to do whatever they want in the name of "freedom." In our opinion, this creates anarchy and not freedom. We believe that if everyone does as he pleases, then each person is concerned only with self-interests and doesn't learn to help or care for others.

For example, we believe that everyone in a family should do chores rather than leaving these for one person (usually Mom!). If a family is a family, then everyone has a part. We also think that paying children for doing chores gives them money under false pretenses. It gives a child a distorted value that everything difficult in life deserves a payment. Unfortunately, this is not how life is in actuality. Instead, chores are a part of everyday living and children need to learn that they will be doing them all their lives. Expecting a reward for a completed chore will lead to bitter disappointment when that child eventually becomes an adult.

In addition to understanding freedom, most of us realize that parenting is a difficult chore and it's harder to do than it was 10 or 15 years ago. We agree with this concept. Many things have affected our society and our families. Children do not respond to the dominant-submissive type relationship which was the typical way of raising children.

Instead, children seek more of a democratic involvement with equality and participation. They see it on T.V., in labor unions, political campaigns, in school, and, hopefully, in their parents. Peaceful co-existence occurs in a family when each person is treated with respect. In other words, each person has a vital and important role within the family.

Sally, a new mother of 12-year-old Tommy, thought that parents need to be bosses and she should never let her "guard" down or else she would get hurt. Right from the start she made sure that Tommy did everything "just right." It was as if Sally were scared that since this was not her biological offspring he would take advantage of her. Through all of this, Tommy appeared confused and resentful that he did all the right things but received little acknowledgement. If he balked at doing a request, he was severely scolded. It seemed Sally could keep the rules but was afraid to get close.

The situation was complicated by the sudden appearance of Sally's 15-year-old son Louis, who had decided to come back and live with his mother. Because of her need not to upset Louis or drive him away, she let him do almost anything he pleased.

This created quite a crisis in the family as both Louis and Tommy started to fight over Sally's love as Tommy saw the basic inequities of the situation. It was through this turmoil that Sally discovered that she needed a more middle- of-the-road approach where both children learned discipline and yet received an adequate amount of love.

We believe that children are social beings and that they want to belong. Their misbehavior is usually a way of being a part of the family even if it's destructive. To us, all behavior has a purpose and sometimes the child wishes to be significant in the family but doesn't know how to do this properly. Establishing a caring environment is important and is one of the necessities in helping reduce misbehavior. In working with families to develop more harmony, we have found several procedures and ideas that may help families in this task. These include:

1. Remember that because children aren't equal in size or intelligence, it doesn't mean they don't deserve equal respect.

2. A person is not a victim of forces beyond his or her control. Everyone makes choices. Because a child is in a stepfamily doesn't mean he's supposed to misbehave or be a problem. We also believe that "not" making a decision is still a decision. You are deciding to stay the same.

3. Children need to be part of the family. Doing everything for children teaches them that all problems will be solved by the parents. Picking up a child's clothes teaches the child that you are a servant and not a parent.

4. Let children be a part of both the fun and work of the family. They can help plan vacations and they can do chores. Hard work teaches resourcefulness.

5. Children need to learn freedom along with responsibility. Letting children do whatever they want leads to chaos. Many of our problem adolescents have no respect for anyone but themselves and their peers. They have been taught selfishness, not responsibility.

6. Encouragement is the key to success, not criticism.

7. Children can be taught to get along and respect their brothers and sisters. Parents must not only teach this, they must live it.

8. Nagging, preaching, and repeating directions are useless activities and contribute to misbehavior. The old axiom, "Actions speak louder than words," is true. Parents need to be consistent.

9. The final decision rests with the parent. Children need to have limits and rules. If you don't parent, no one else will.

10. Competition makes enemies of every fellow human. Competitive children strive for success because they believe only in themselves and do not care what others are doing. Children need to learn to cooperate and not compete in the family.

Of course, reading what to do is much simpler than knowing how to do it. Parents have a large part in a family's success and can do several things which can help guarantee a happier family and less hassles for all involved.

We believe that guiding and helping a child is much more effective than punishment. Show a child how to become involved and support him for mistakes as well as successes. Too often parents are extremely critical and forget that making mistakes is a great way to learn. Adults are so perfection-oriented that they want to be good at everything even if they've never done it before.

Give a child a new task, help them with it, but let the "child" do most of the work. After they have learned, let them experiment. True, they may break a few things, but they also will grow in self-confidence.

All of us like responsibility. As an adult, you like to be given the opportunity to show your talents if you feel good about yourself. Let your children have the same chance. Encourage them for their talents and initiative. Many great persons have failed. They'll be in good company.

Besides strong encouragement and support, make your child become a part of the family. Don't get caught up in male and female stereotypes. Boys can learn to cook and clean and girls can play sports. Open up your horizons so your children can reach their highest potentials. All of us are lazy and procrastinate, so if you have to push a child at first to become a part, do so. If children learn to contribute from the beginning, it is much easier than starting at 9, 13, or 17 years of age.

Explain to the child that each person has a part and if one doesn't contribute, everyone suffers. Of course that means the parents can't sit idly on the couch watching. Make clean-up days a family event.

If a child refused to perform a task, find a suitable consequence that is not physical punishment or excess verbiage. We believe that all children misbehave, and usually a reprimand or discussion will stop the action from occurring in the future. However, if it occurs on a regular basis, something has to be done.

This is what we call a logical consequence. For this to be effective, several rules must be followed. First, you need to sit down with the child and examine the action and what harm it is causing to the child and others. Next, you must inform the child that if the action continues, certain consequences will occur. It is not to be discussed in great detail or used as punishment. Rather, you must seek to find a consequence which fits into the action. When the misbehavior occurs after you have done all these steps, you simply verbally recognize the action and employ the consequence. You do not get into arguments or sit and discuss the action ad nauseum.

For instance, Johnny had trouble feeding the dog. He never seemed to fill the bowl and Mom always had to do it. A simple consequence helped with this misbehavior. Johnny was told to feed the dog before he ate dinner. It was explained that dogs need to eat just like Johnny or they will die. If Johnny "forgot" to feed the dog, he wouldn't get dinner either. Of course, he tested this out and Mom stuck to her guns. Johnny didn't eat nor get a snack later when he cried and yelled that he was hungry. Within three days, his misbehavior was gone. Johnny's Mom did not sit down and discuss that the dog was dying (like she used to!)

or scream and get angry. Instead, she didn't feed Johnny or give in to his whims. In fact, she taught Johnny two valuable lessons. It's not nice to starve animals and if you want a pet, you need to take care of it.

The same principle can work with the child who leaves her clothes all over the floor. Either Mom can leave them there or put them in a sack for a few weeks. Pretty soon the child will have to go to school naked. For some reason, the child soon learns to pick up her clothes.

The list could be endless, but it is vitally important that the parents agree on the consequences and stick together. If the child can play one parent against the other, it will not work.

The modeling of the parents as a marital couple can also teach children many values. A couple that belittles, criticizes, and complains teaches these values to the children. Partners need to show caring, love, and respect. Be willing to help each other and praise actions. Deal with conflicts constructively and with a sense of humor. Be positive and encourage group discussion of important family matters. In our world of tension and stress, this can be hard to do. It takes work and commitment. We also believe that children don't need to be servants to parents. For instance, Mom and Dad are visiting with friends at home while their children are all playing next door. The baby is with the parents but it is past his bedtime, so he is beginning to be bothersome. Dad yells for one of the older kids to take the baby for a stroll. The child agrees to do so with a sigh of regret.

In actuality, this was an unreasonable request. Parents shouldn't ask of children what they themselves wouldn't do. Since Dad was with friends, he took advantage of his child's compliance rather than put the baby to bed as he should have.

Rudolph Driekurs, in a book entitled <u>Discipline Without Tears</u>, provides some important behavior and clues to success in a family. He states that parents should communicate in these ways:

1. Avoid discouragement. Work for improvement, not perfection.
2. Commend effort and build on strengths.
3. Separate the "action done" from the doer. Because children do something wrong doesn't mean they are bad children.
4. Failure is not one's worth but one's lack of skill. Show faith.
5. Let a child move at his or her own speed. Stimulate, don't push.
6. Integrate the child into the family.
7. Don't praise. Some children only work for this special recognition. Encourage.
8. Give opportunities to the discouraged child, not just to those who are responsible.
9. Solicit the help of family members with a misbehaving child.
10. Be optimistic.

Even with these tips for helping a family become closer, it still takes time. We know that there are boundaries in the stepfamily which must be worked through. Family members need to learn to treat each other with respect and as they themselves wish to be treated. If you can begin this process, love will soon start to appear. It's hard for us not to like someone that likes us. Many times children will have trouble getting close to a new parent and strokes may be few and far between. Even if they get close, they may have a backlash or a strong negative reaction moments later. It's not unusual for a child to laugh and play a game with you one minute and tell you "you're not my real parent" the next. Certainly, this hurts one's feelings but it is easier to understand when you know the child is struggling.

As a new Mom, Susan was having trouble keeping Brenda in tow. Whenever she went to the supermarket, she would leave Brenda in the car so that she could have an easier time of shopping. Susan would tell Brenda that she would bring her some type of present.

Soon Brenda began to realize the effects of "bribing" and demanded material offerings as a reward for being good. Susan forgot that if you bribe a child for good behavior, you are showing that you do not trust the child and are actually discouraging this person.

We believe that children want to be good and have a desire to belong and contribute. Children need to see the advantages of cooperating and being part of a family rather than asking, "What's in it for me?". Pretty soon the appetite of material gain grows monstrous, and a child believes the world owes him everything. If the child doesn't get what he wants, he will punish. "I'll show them!" As many parents continue to reward children with material things, they deny them the basic satisfactions of living ... how to contribute and be useful in our world.

It's important right from the beginning in the stepfamily that the past is eliminated as much as possible and that the family work on its own memories: take trips together, go fishing, watch special movies, make puzzles, and do a hundred other things that bring memories and moments of enjoyment. Sitting and staring at a T.V. doesn't help you get close. Share in the child's activities and go to their special and "not so special" events. Be with them to share their miseries and joys.

Some shared activities we have found effective are these:

1. Do house cleaning together and celebrate afterward.
2. Have the kids take you out to dinner. If need be, give them money beforehand.
3. Eat your meals together, especially dinner. Use the time to communicate and share. Many troubled families never seem to share a meal and feel uneasy sitting together.
4. Play games and activities together. Play football, badminton, make puzzles, or try Monopoly.
5. Share your work and find out what the kids do in school. Read their school reports and papers.

Establishing a philosophy of family isn't easy. Developing an open atmosphere where concerns can be aired and dealt with without criticism is hard for most of us and takes a lot of work. In the stepfamily, many times parents did not feel like they were successful in their families during the first marriage and so place pressure on themselves to make it right this time. Usually they continue the same old patterns with the end results being the same. Modeling, teaching, involvement, caring, and encouragement can be your most effective tools for success. We have found very positive results through using them. We encourage you to do the same.

Understanding Children's Behavior
in the Stepfamily

Raising a child in any family is difficult and the stepfamily is no exception. Most parents want to teach a child self-discipline, but often the adult's behavior reinforces dependence and self-gratification in the child rather than self-reliance.

It is our belief that most children are a lot smarter than parents give them credit for being. Kids act according to how they size up a situation and their behavior is a reflection of those perceptions. We would like to explore some basic guidelines for "why" children exhibit certain inappropriate behaviors and what parents can do to eliminate and reduce these negative actions.

As adults, you can influence a person's behavior but only under extreme circumstances can you control attitudes and behavior. We like to point out to people that the only way to get others to do what you want is to put a gun to their head and even then people will resist. The best way to affect a person's behavior is how you act as a parent and what you do. In other words, changing your behavior opens new alternatives to a child, and thus new behaviors, in a particular situation. Thus, if the child is not cooperating no matter how much you ask, beg, plead, joke, or spank, then what you are doing is probably contributing to the negative behavior rather than ending it. At that point, it would make sense to try something different.

What occurs in this situation is that few parents know what to do next. Having exhausted what they consider to be all their possibilities, a parent may resort to physical force in order to control a child.

It seems to us that many parents are experiencing trouble with their children and are becoming increasingly upset. It seems like the old ways to raise children do not work anymore and that traditions for child-raising are now being ignored.

In fact, many people complain that the behavior of children is deplorable in our society. Children seem noisy, inconsiderate, and unmannerly. They often show a disrespect for parents and all elders and may actually insult them. It is not unusual to see children misbehave in public places by crying, having temper tantrums, demanding special treats, and constantly asking for more money. Parents plead, punish, and bribe to get some tranquility. So how has all this come about?

Several child experts believe that democracy as a way of life has forced many changes in our society. Americans believe in equality, and this has transformed our society and our parenting patterns. Everyone has a chance and nobody "rules" over the other. It used to be that the father ruled the whole family, including the woman. This is often no longer the case. With women's rights, the husband has lost power over his wife and it seems that many parents have lost control over their children.

This push for equality has happened in such areas of society as management and labor, racial issues, federal government employees, and numerous other situations. When we speak of equality in families, we do not mean that children have equal knowledge or experience as adults but rather that they have equal claims to dignity and respect.

This is sometimes difficult for parents to understand, for they may wish to be superior. The "you do as I say" philosophy is becoming ineffective with children as they become more exposed to democratic living as shown on the media, in school, and with friends. Children are maturing quicker and are exposed to a greater number of experiences than parents may realize.

For example, the child in the stepfamily may experience many situations that may mature the child "beyond his or her years." Marie Winn, in her book <u>Children Without Childhood</u>, points out that society has changed its fundamental attitudes toward children. Rather than protecting children from life's troubles, parents are preparing them for the battle. This ideology focuses on the concept that children must be exposed early to adult experiences so that they may be ready for the cruel world.

We believe that this attitude may make a child's life even more difficult and confusing beyond what occurs in normal developmental processes.

There are many factors that have contributed to difficulties in raising children and listed below are just a few:

1. The rising divorce rate and emergence of nontraditional family forms.

2. Poor economic conditions which have caused single parents to struggle for survival and children to work.
3. Dual-career families and the decrease in family time.
4. The advent of T.V. It seems as a passive babysitter for parents and a distribution of massive uncensored material for children.
5. The availability of drugs and the ability to buy them.
6. A sexual society that preoccupies itself with constant titillation and encourages experimentation at a young age.

Some experts are disagreeing as to whether children can handle the type of difficulties they encounter nowadays and indicate that modern children need to be more sheltered. Indeed, children seem to be begging nowaways for more adult- like activities and yet still appear to have difficulty assuming maturer responsibilities.

Defining what limits and experiences are important for a child may be vitally important for the parents in a stepfamily. This child will be forced to experience adult responsibilities possibly at a tender age. Coping with divorce, befriending confused parents, and assuming adult roles in a single-parent family may be but a few of the circumstances that could differ this child from other peers.

While having these experiences can widen the psychological and emotional scope of a child, it is important that parents protect the child, assume the burden for difficulties, and enable the child to receive experiences when he or she can handle them. We believe that stepfamily parents need to assume a child's capabilities by remembering what it was like for them when they were 6, 8, or 15 years of age, or possibly how they wanted it to be. As parents, you cannot change many experiences that a child will face in a stepfamily but you can help alleviate some of the conflict and pain. Being thoughtful of what the child needs to know may be sound advice. In other words, for a child to hear and know everything you do and say may not be helpful. Sometimes "secrets" are a good thing.

We find it frightening that some parents believe that a child must "experience" everything so that he or she has no questions or doubts. This type of parent will drag a kid to divorce court to see the process or explain how every piece of furniture was divided. Others will involve their children in long custody battles and expect things to be normal afterwards.

On the other hand, parents sometimes expect children to act like adults when instead they need the "right" to be immature. This means that a child may be hostile or more excitable and unpredictable than you, but that is okay. It is an adult fallacy that if you explain something to children, they will understand it. They may just need time or may not be developmentally ready. For example, a six-year- old girl may not be willing to hug the new Dad, while a nine- year-old, who is more wanting to please men, may readily agree. If the new Dad feels instantly rejected, he is setting himself up for some hard times.

While attempting to balance equality and yet providing an appropriate atmosphere for the child, the issues of freedom and responsibility become important.

To us, democracy does not mean that people do as they please but rather that people respect the freedom of others. If no one respects each other, then you have anarchy, not democracy.

So we believe that democracy implies a sense of order which entails restrictions, obligations, and responsibilities. This order is not just for individual benefit; instead it helps everyone. Too often parents let children have all the freedom but none of the responsibilities. Thus, the parent becomes the slave and the child is the master. Without restrictions, children lose a sense of self, of right and wrong, and do not learn the necessities of living in a society. With structured limits, a child develops a sense of security and worth. Without them, you have spoiled brats.

The job of parents is to stimulate and encourage children into being a part of society and the human race without demanding submission and forcing compliance. To do this, we feel certain principles must be understood:

1. Children want to belong--even if Johnny misbehaves, he still wants to be a part of the family group. From their successes, children learn how to behave and they draw conclusions from what they do. While "belonging" is a basic goal, a child will try many methods to achieve this goal.

2. Behavior is goal-directed--right or wrong, a child will do what gives him or her a place and will abandon behavior that makes the child feel left out. However, how children think they belong and what behavior they do to achieve that goal may not always be understood by either child or parent.

3. Children are excellent observers but are erratic interpreters. They often draw incorrect conclusions and thus pick incorrect behavior to win their place.

For instance, Joan was happy when she found that she would have a younger new sister to live and play with her. Instantly she volunteered to help clothe her and take care of her. Mom refused her offers and soon she realized that Mom was giving her new sister all the attention. After a few weeks a problem developed as Joan began to "copy" the baby behaviors and would soil clothes and even start temper tantrums. Of course Joan received lots of attention but not quite what she expected. However, punishment was better than no attention at all.

4. A child's environment prepares him or her for life's accomplishments and difficulties. Sometimes a child with a handicap will become highly successful while others will give up. We believe a child can choose how to face problems.

Another important component of the environment is the family atmosphere. A child will absorb the basic values and morals of a family. If parents are understanding and tolerant of others, then children will usually feel the same.

As we have mentioned in previous chapters, the relationship of the parents will set the model for all the relationships in the family. If the parents stress cooperation, this will be the general rule of thumb rather than competition. If the parents are hostile and constantly vie for dominance, the children will attack and attempt to overpower each other. If all the children have a trait in common, this trait is what signifies the general family atmosphere.

Equally important in the stepfamily is the positioning of the children in the family. With a stepfamily, each child tries to vie for a position and this may be very confusing when different sets of children are added to the family. Not only must a child contend with competing with his siblings but added family members may confuse and even aggravate established patterns. A stepfamily needs to be able to adjust and sometimes the children may be reluctant.

Larry, a 12-year-old and the first born of the family, enjoyed his role as the leader of the children and the perfect child. He set the standards and the rest of the children had to live up to them. When Dad remarried, his new wife, Evelyn, brought her three teenagers with the family. Now Larry was fourth in line and he resented it. In order to assume dominance, he bossed his brothers and sisters more than ever, but they resisted. In order to gain attention and power, Larry started to have huge arguments with his step-Mom and eventually began experimenting with drugs.

It is helpful to remember that children seek a place in the family and that if parents are aware, they can help a child. Typically, middle children have difficulty competing with an older sibling because they always seem a step behind. Younger children may tend to be spoiled or become helpless as others "wait" on them. Remembering a child's position in the family can be advantageous for parents if used correctly.

5. Encouragement rather than discouragement is the most useful parenting technique. To us, a child that displays maladaptive behavior is doing so out of discouragement. Children who believe they are failures and doubt their abilities are our problem children. It is sad to us that sometimes stepfamilies give up on children. Maybe they were angry about the divorce, ignored by a single parent, or feel like they are second rate in the family. Too often these messages are confirmed by a parent's focus on the negative.

It is too common a phenomenon that parents do not recognize and encourage their children. Even our society is negatively oriented. Our newspapers and T.V. talk about what's wrong with our world with little advice for improvement. To prove our point, when we do workshops we ask people to list 10 positive and 10 negative attributes. The negative list is quickly finished while most people flounder on the positive. The same thing happens when we ask couples to describe the best things about their mates and their children.

By encouraging children we do not mean to shelter them from life but rather to face it. As adults, parents know that pain is a part of life and so it must be for the child. Feeling sorry for someone hinders rather than helps him.

Rather, it is vital to encourage a child toward independence. An attitude that says, "You will make it and you're okay with me." If a child fails, encourage him or her to try again or share techniques that can help success. Help a child rely on strengths rather than weaknesses. Teach a child to work for improvement.

We believe it is also helpful to have some methods for working with children that are misbehaving or do not know how to belong.

Dr. Tom Sweeney, in his book, <u>Adlerian Counseling</u>, relates that cooperation, not conformity, should be the goal between parents and children. Children need to participate in the labors of daily living. Sometimes parents ignore this by doing everything for the child or by assigning tasks to a youngster that they would not do themselves. Dr. Sweeney gives six guidelines for parents in working with children.

1. Free yourself of the mistaken notion that you should "control" the child's behavior.
2. Accept responsibility for changing your behavior first rather than the child's.
3. Respect children for making the choices they can under the circumstances as they perceive them.
4. Realize that children are attempting to make a place for themselves by whatever means seem available to them (a useful or useless behavior).
5. Understand that when children misbehave, it is an outward sign of their internal discouragement as participating members of your family.
6. Commit yourself to helping children learn self-discipline and cooperation by friendly participation in the daily tasks everyone must fulfill.

Basically, children's disruptive behavior can be categorized into four distinct methods or goals. These goals are what children expect to achieve by their behaviors, whether consciously or unconsciously.

1. Attention seeking: While everyone does seek attention, this child constantly annoys others. This person believes "I only count when I am being noticed or served." The attention-oriented child's behavior is either active or passive in orientation. Active actions include the child that bothers others, shows off, performs minor mischief, constantly asks questions, clowns, and generally keeps everyone busy.

   The passive child is shy, uptight, says I can't, may have speech problems, messy, worries, and gets others to do things so he or she won't have to do it.

   Most parents fall into several traps with these children. They punish, nag, coax, remind often, advise, and give service. When this is done, the child will receive attention and stop the action temporarily. Soon thereafter the child will resume the behavior or disturb in another way.

   We recommend rather than nagging that the parent ignore the child or do the unexpected. Above all things, do not show your annoyance. Be firm with this child and give lots of attention when the child is performing correct behavior rather than negative actions.

2. Power seeking: Children discover very early that they can say "no." Some are actively stubborn and adults usually realize they are being challenged. The power-seeking child believes "I only count when I am dominating, when you do what I want you to do."

Active actions include arguing, contradicting, continuing forbidden acts, temper tantrums, dishonesty, and goofing off.

The passive child tends to be lazy, stubborn, forgetful, and does little work.

Besides being challenged by this child, most adults feel threatened and may tend to be "preachy."

If you get into a conflict with the power-oriented child, you're in trouble. Normally the action will intensify because the child wants to be the boss. It is better to recognize and admit that the child has power. This is important because this child has a fear of being overpowered.

We believe that parents need to be firm and maintain order. This does not mean engaging in a power struggle and certainly not showing anger. Rather, being consistent with <u>actions</u> and not <u>talk</u> is a prime prerequisite for success. Remember that proper behavior is stimulated, not demanded. If a child has all that energy to be argumentative, surely he or she can use that energy in a more constructive manner.

For example, many parents will beg a child to go to bed. In an apparently mysterious manner, the child's favorite T.V. show always seems to be at bedtime hour. If not, the child may substitute an activity that "cannot be stopped." As the parent yells, the child resists and may cry. No matter what the consequence, if the child stays up, he or she wins.

In contrast, a firm parent states the bedtime hour much earlier in the day so that it is known. There are no exceptions. The child is tucked in (usually resistingly) at the assigned hour and kissed goodnight. After this, whatever the child says or does is ignored. The parents act as if the child is not really there. By withdrawing, the child finds the battlefield empty. We have found that within a week the child will go to bed at bedtime in an effort to cooperate.

3. Revenge: The revengeful child is very difficult to work with. His message to everyone is "I can't be liked. I count if I can hurt others as much as I hurt."

Active actions by this child include cruelty, stealing, bedwetting, fighting, and being a sore loser. Passively, this child displays moodiness, rebellion, threatening behavior, and may be withdrawn.

Parents of this type of child usually feel deeply hurt, which is exactly what the child wants. If you punish or seek retaliation, it will produce rebellion.

Rather, you must retain order with minimum restraint and show this child that he or she is liked and that you will want to spend time with him or her.

4. Inadequacy: This child says "I can't do anything right and I'm no good; so I won't do anything at all."

Being very passive, children like this give up, rarely participate, and project a helpless image.

Most parents throw up their hands and give up. "I don't know what to do" is a common response.

Rather than giving up with this child, eliminate all criticism. Encourage any positive step no matter how small. Don't give pity to this child if he or she is disappointed. Disappointments are a way of life. Focus on the child's strengths and not weaknesses.

Besides understanding the basic motives or actions of a child, it is worthwhile to understand the basic reactions of new children to a remarriage and a stepfamily. This blending of family cultures can be difficult. After all, the decisions of divorce and remarriage are those of the adults of the family and the children usually do not have a large say in the situation.

Young and Pre-School Children

We have found children of this age to be very adaptable if the parents are concerned and willing to work for the welfare of the child. If there is a large amount of animosity between ex-spouses, the child may become confused and depressed.

When a child is very young, a caring new parent can fill the void of a natural parent and a close relationship can be established. However, the concepts of divorce and remarriage will be difficult for the child to understand and he or she may mourn the loss of a parent longer than an adult would.

Parents must be observable and notice any immature behavior, because the child may seek attention and caring by retreating to baby-like behavior.

If contact with the non-custodial parent is not very good, the child may be resentful, begin to blame himself or herself for the divorce or think that the parent doesn't want to relate.

The most important thing to do with pre-schoolers is to listen to them, answer questions sincerely, and show love to the child from __all__ parents. If the child feels accepted and a part of the family, separations, new brothers and sisters, or new households are much easier to accept. A child of this age seeks caring and stability, something the stepfamily needs to, and can, provide.

Elementary School-Age Children

Children at this age can be very interesting. Their emotions are easily seen and shown and this may cause parents some difficulties. Girls at this age are usually close to their mothers and strongly model many of the parents' behaviors. They are identifying their sexuality and may even compete for the attention of a new father. Sometimes they will be quite vocal (usually more than boys) and express what is on their minds.

We have found some girls of this age may grow up too fast and assume roles beyond their capabilities, especially with single fathers. In this regard the child may become almost a type of girlfriend and become party to adult expectations. This can be trouble, especially when Dad starts dating. Keeping role expectations of a child at a normal developmental level is important, especially when a remarriage occurs and the adult may want to fill in some emotional or conversational gaps with a child.

Boys tend to identify more with fathers and usually are proud of their accomplishments, new girfriends. While they may be less vocal, boys also may be angry or confused about the remarriage and stepfamily.

Children of this age expect the world to be "fair and just" and will want the house to be run accordingly. They need structure and will test whatever rules you put forth. If there were problems with the child before the remarriage, things may get worse.

One important element at this time is to make sure the child knows what is expected and allow for emotional discussions. Just like pre-school children, these kids may also be slow in grieving for a parent. Even though adults have moved on to new relationships, the child may still be confused, especially if the non-custodial parent is seen on an infrequent basis. Sometimes in these circumstances, children get very defensive and may idolize the missing parent. They may also show anger at the step-parent because he or she is around and reminds them of the biological parent.

Teenagers

This group is difficult for parents when things are perfect rather than when things are changing. Teenagers like things "their way" and usually do not want their lives disturbed. They are "I" centered and interested basically in themselves, as a general rule.

One problem we encounter frequently is that parents will give the choice of major decisions to the teenage child. In other words, the teenager is considered a full adult. We believe this is a mistake. Remembering how you were as a teenager may help you gain a perspective on the situation.

For example, many teenagers choose the parent whom they will live with after a divorce. While input in this matter is good, the capacity of a teenager to make this adult (and very difficult) decision should be analyzed. Who can best determine the welfare of a child, the parent or the child? Hopefully, it is the parent.

Since teenagers are caught in the middle of a developmental struggle (am I adult or child?), they may hassle and argue in an effort to assert their freedom. They also may make some obvious mistakes and may lack a mature sense of judgment.

If the teenager is given freedom to do whatever he or she wants, the new step-parent may be in for some difficult encounters. Feelings and words can get way out of hand as the teenager's life gets more and more frustrating.

It is also a difficult time for parents in a stepfamily. Again, we believe that a step-parent who helps support the child and spends time with the child on an every-day basis needs to be recognized by a parental title rather than Sam or Sue. Teenagers may be the most resistant people to this type of suggestion.

While determining a proper balance between freedom and structure is important, the integration of children from two sets of families may also be paramount. Teenagers of the opposite sex may have sexual feelings and sometimes these attractions occur with a new spouse. It is generally a good idea to discuss these things openly so that everyone involved knows what is occurring and that they are not abnormal.

In summary, teenagers are typically in a developmental crisis in any type of family and so the stepfamily must understand that everything that happens is not all "their" fault. Helping teenagers understand what is happening and finding a place for them in the family is of primary importance in successful stepfamilies.

Adult Children

While you may expect the adult child to be more understanding of your dilemmas, he or she may not. This rejection of a new spouse or a stepfamily is not unusual.

Amy, a woman in her forties, relates her story in a typical fashion. "When I left John, I felt very confused and guilty. I sought help and acceptance from my parents and children and everyone seemed to be obliging. My son was stationed in Europe and he felt that if I thought what I was doing was okay, then he would support me. My mother also agreed. The problem came when I called my son in Houston. He got very angry and literally began yelling at me. It was very confusing to me and I got angry myself. Of all my children, I thought he would understand more than his brother. I guess I was wrong. Finally I told him that I was going to do what I wanted anyway even if he didn't like it. I'm not going to let him bring me down. So, we haven't talked in a long time and now that I'm remarried, he is even more resentful."

It doesn't have to be this way, but always expecting adult children to understand may be misguided. However, if the adult child does not accept your actions, it does not always mean this child will be this way. Sometimes time and discussion will help iron things out. In dealing with an adult child, there might be some things to keep in mind:

1. Tell them when you're ready.

2. Be honest but reveal what you think is worthy of discussion.

3. Understand. They may be upset. After all, you are disturbing their world regarding holidays, phone calls, and many other things.

4. If they feel bad for an ex-spouse, let them feel it. Don't try to deny or convince them to feel otherwise.

5. Expect resistance to a new spouse or children.

6. Assure them that you love them.

With the adult child it is important to be truthful, and yet it is vital that you understand that the adult child may not always agree with what is best for you.

The Effects of Relatives, Professionals
and Society on the Stepfamily

A major hassle for members of a stepfamily is that everyone wants to have a piece of your life. It is hard to understand <u>how</u> this happens but it does.

Problems often begin before the remarriage. In the divorce proceedings, relationships among both the nuclear and extended family become strained. By the time legal battles have ended, little consideration for ex-spouses or "that side" of the family is left. We have seen this occur even when spouses thought they were friends. Lawyers will make the division of property very difficult, and before you realize what is occurring everyone is fighting.

Children may also be used as a pawn in this game. Many spouses will say that they will do "anything for the kids" but the majority of decisions are made for their own self- interest.

In fact, we have seen custody decisions made on the basis of self-interest rather than for the child, and eventually everyone suffers. This is why we believe that single- custody decisions are a much better option for most families than joint custody. It is our belief that joint custody is usually arranged for the parents and not for the child's benefit. This is in direct contrast to many other human service professionals, who constantly harp about joint custody as the only option for divorcing couples. To us, they do not realize the ramifications and harm joint custody can cause most children and the superior skills that parents must have in order for it to work effectively. We rarely see the communicative and caring skills that are necessary for this elaborate procedure and even most therapists, who themselves are involved in joint custody, have trouble making it work.

Some of the problems we have seen with joint custody include these:

1. Kids are shuttled back and forth between houses like furniture. This appears fine when the child is young, but it soon becomes a problem when the child reaches school age. Even young children soon resent not being able to stay in one place or when they wish to be with their friends. We have observed that children who bounce like this spend the greater part of their time with the parent and often have trouble making friends with children their own age.

2. Parents find that half their week is totally or abnormally involved with entertaining the child and they may resent it. As children begin school, they become involved in school activities and usually seek one stable situation and do not like moving around.

3. Ex-spouses need to be able to talk and communicate with each other at a very friendly level. But now they are constantly arranging times and pickups. While this is not only difficult

but painful for many people, it can become a more precarious situation when one person remarries. Remarried families and joint custody are indeed an odd combination. It is often hard enough to figure things out without having to involve a new spouse in the family circus. Sometimes therapists can also help; matters like this get way out of hand. For example, we heard of one therapist that recommended that the kids have the house and that the parents move in and out. They would change monthly as one would live in an apartment and the other in the house. Each month, they would switch places. This seemed great in theory, but the kids soon learned to take advantage of the situation and behaved like they were poor deprived children. Also, one of the spouses remarried and didn't enjoy paying "rent" to the ex-spouse. In addition to all of this, the ex-spouses had trouble keeping any relationships because they thought they were traveling salespersons.

4. Parents have to live near each other for years at a time. This can be difficult since the average American family moves every three years. If adults are to make this work, they often have to give up important career opportunities. If both spouses are very career-oriented, joint custody will take up too much of their time and the children will end up staying with baby-sitters or alone in the "moving" house.

When a remarriage occurs, relationships can be even more difficult. Problems such as integrating ex-spouses, taking care of children in two families, dealing with old and new grandparents, or other extended family can become quite a chore. Besides understanding them, you also have to hear all persons' opinions and what they want from both you and members of your family. That is why many stepfamilies feel like they are being pushed and torn in a hundred directions.

Sometimes, extended family members can help split a family apart. Jackie, a new mother of three, felt caught in the middle. "It seems like everyone always wanted to tell us what to do. It's hard enough with two sets of grandparents but we had four sets that were very vocal. They each were bossy and demanded to have the children for vacations and holidays. It got to be so ridiculous that Phil and I argued all the time. It wasn't until I left for a while that we started to set our own priorities."

In addition to family members, people tend to form new relationships or break old ones with friends from the past. After a divorce you lose contact with many friends who were an important part of your life.

It seems that single individuals have trouble keeping relationships with couples. It's easy to understand the ambivalence and uncertainty of other people. For instance, married couples suddenly bring the children along on dinner dates with you rather than hiring a babysitter. At the same time, you start to develop new friends who are usually in the same circumstances as you.

So when you get married, it's hard to keep the single friends. So you have gained married friends, lost married friends, gained single friends, and lost single friends. And, when you get remarried, you may well look for friends who are in similar circumstances. That's why stepfamilies often look for friends who have been through divorce, people who can understand. Most therapists know that the majority of help in our country comes from the informal network people establish with friends and relatives. They help us put our world into perspective. In fact, we have found that couples who have the most trouble in their marriages lack these informal networks. They are all alone and lose perspective of what it's like to care for someone.

We believe it's also important to keep some friends that are separate. In other words, many couples depend on each other for constant support in a relationship. Now that both partners are usually working, both men and women have opportunities to share and establish ties with different types of people. Rather than taking away from a relationship, individual friendships can enhance a person and bring added interest to a marriage relationship. Thus, a balance of mutual and individual friends can provide important emotional support systems to people rather than overburdening a spouse.

In general, society and culture can have a large impact on the stepfamily. If you know what to expect, it can help you, but it may not reduce your anger. Stepfamilies are given messages that they are second best and that their children will not "turn out" to be like other kids. Nobody has proved this in research, but it makes people feel more secure if they can say it.

There are so many influences upon a child that it's difficult to say which have the most impact. We do know that good caring families are helpful to both children and adults. We think it's easier when there are both male and female role models for a child, but single parents are also doing an admirable job in many cases. Stepfamilies can provide a valuable support system for children and help them to become responsible and contributing adults. Like any family system, strong families have a better chance of reaching this goal than troubled ones.

In coping with societal influences, there are certain groups which have a direct impact on the stepfamily. These include:

1. <u>Lawyers</u>--It seems that whatever you do or change in a stepfamily, it has something to do with a lawyer. Most folks in stepfamilies feel as though they're supporting lawyers for life. They also believe everything that lawyers tell them and may not want to make decisions without their advice. This may be costly both to your pocketbook and your relationships. Lawyers work on the adversary system and this can be detrimental to relationships. They want to win and you may just be looking for a solution. Some people say that our lawyers never do preventive work, they only deal with problems after they occur. In addition to this philosophy, lawyers keep on creating more and more rules so that you have to use their services whether you want to or not. In fact, other countries like Japan have one-third as many lawyers as the United States, and three times the number of engineers. Their philosophy is that engineers contribute and progress the society while lawyers just haggle.

   If you have an understanding of what lawyers are supposed to do, then you can use them to your advantage rather than disadvantage. We have seen too many families who create their own problems because of legal hassles. Some typical examples of conflict are these:

- demanding outrageous child support payments or demanding money constantly from an ex-spouse
- allowing ex-spouses too much freedom in seeing a child or too little time
- endlessly negotiating over senseless items for years and years
- letting an ex-spouse run roughshod over you without consulting a lawyer
- staying in one place or one job because a lawyer says to do it
- never getting a second opinion on controversial matters
- keeping a lawyer that isn't providing you good services
- never negotiating items that have changed
- getting over self-pride and your lawyer's advice when you know a different decision would help the child
- failure to seek legal advice when your child's mental, physical, or emotional health is in danger
- failing to provide the best life for you and your family even if it entails legal hassles.

An example of this would be the dilemmas of Jack and Jill. After a divorce, Jack is supposed to pay a small amount of child support for their son. He chooses to live nearby and since visitation is not clearly stated, he visits as he pleases even when Jill has a date with her. Within a few months, child support becomes an obsolete item because Jack can't seem to make ends meet. However, he continues to see their son as much as he wishes.

After approximately two years, Jill remarries. Joe becomes actively involved as a new father. For all concerned he wishes to adopt Jill's son because of his love and his continued financial support. Jill approaches Jack with the idea and he defiantly says "no way." Jill then seeks a lawyer to determine her rights because of nonpayment of child support money. Jack proceeds to get a lawyer and the fight begins all over again.

We believe that lawyers provide a very valuable function in our society. Our only caution is that you use this service for your benefit and not because someone else is telling you what to do. You can make decisions without the help of a lawyer if you try to keep past and present relationships on a friendly note. Acting as a mature and caring adult models important behavior for your children. Ranting and screaming while pushing for revenge leads to disastrous results for you and the children. Lawyers need to understand this point of view and only you can tell them. If you feel that they are not on your side, hire another one. There are plenty for all of us.

2. <u>School Systems</u>--Most schools are cooperative with difficulties that you may have. We have previously talked about using your new name with your child even if it is not "legally" changed. This would be something that is decided by you and the individual school district. Sometimes we place the school in the middle of our family problems. For example, an ex-spouse may decide to observe a child in school without informing anyone

and this may make everyone a bit anxious. Picking a child up after school without informing a parent can create quite a controversy, particularly if no one knows about it.

Teacher-parent meetings can become quite involved for the stepfamily. We have seen sets of ex-spouses and stepfamily parents arguing about "their" child's education while the teacher is helplessly stuck in between. Issues like these need to be resolved before they occur. Bringing family problems into the school and using this arena as a battleground can be hopeless for all involved.

Meg, a new mother of two, agrees. "I used to blame everyone for our problems: my ex-husband, the teacher, the school, etc. It wasn't until I realized that I had to get things together in our family that Judy started to change. She was just acting out because her Dad and I were having problems and I was too blind to see. She was receiving the hurt that should have been between her Dad and I."

Schools can also contribute their share of the problem. They may not like the inconvenience of all these "parents" and refuse to help by not sending each parent materials and other data. In school, treating the child as someone who is damaged or different does not help the self- concept of the child and may be less help and more detrimental. This is what is sometimes wrong with special groups or programs for children of divorced parents or of new children. They are treated as if they are not as good or competent as the other children. While we agree that it is important to help children with problems and provide opportunities to share difficulties, it is not always a good idea to stigmatize kids by setting up special groups. This is one of the inherent problems with special education in America.

On the other hand, if you are having difficulties at home with a child, let the school know. Possibly they can be of help and may be able to tell you if the same behavior is occurring in the classroom. Our only caution is that you choose a teacher that respects stepfamilies and their intricacies. A teacher that is biased about stepfamilies can do you and your child a lot of harm. In most cases, school teachers have a good intuitive sense about a child's family. Create a good impression by visiting with them and volunteering your help.

3. <u>Grandparents and Relatives</u>--Although grandparents do not have visitation rights, they do have a large impact on the stepfamily in many cases. Here's a dilemma that many parents have to consider: Are the grandparents and relatives taking the stepfamily's development into consideration, or are they seeking to gratify personal needs? For instance, grandparents of ex-spouses may demand equal time with the child even after a divorce. This often creates problems and keeps alive old family messages. Trying to be nice can sometimes create problems. Rather than insisting that past relatives see children on the ex-spouse's time, you may feel free to share the stepfamily's time. This can be agreeable to the family if they feel comfortable with this choice. However,

most stepfamilies wish to identify with the new grandparents rather than the ex-spouse's. With custody and visitation, it is very hard for many families to get the time that they need and so they resent relatives taking the children away. Often grandparents do not realize that couples work very hard and wish to spend summers and vacation times with their children rather than sending them to relatives. Also, the parents of the ex-spouse may not be supportive of your new family and may say things that are not very agreeable to you. Problems like this can cause great friction and the best way to deal with them is to let an ex-spouse share his or her time, rather than yours.

Another hassle with close relations and grandparents is both overt and subtle nonacceptance of the stepfamily and the new spouse. Actions and words may not fit together and anger may develop on either side of the family. Some examples of common occurrences are these:

- expecting grandparents to immediately accept the new family, which is often unrealistic
- a spouse's parents saying they enjoy a new spouse and yet ignoring this person or condemning every action
- moaning during holidays about how lonely your ex-spouse is
- relatives contriving to keep close relationships with an ex-spouse when it can be damaging to the new family
- refusing to understand how vacations are much different than before

- relatives bringing up the past and reminiscing about old times at family gatherings
- relatives calling you or the kids by your "old" name.

It is important that a spouse has a "family discussion" with his or her parents after the marriage. There are often many items that can keep hanging on for years until they are discussed openly and without reprisal. Every child wants a parent to accept one's decisions but this is not always the case. If parents choose not to support the stepfamily, they have that right. However, it also gives you the right to change your relationship with them. Relatives who are detrimental to the stepfamily can cause great damage since they are aware of old family "secrets" and weaknesses. When they are not supportive of your decisions, we generally advise families to curtail the relationship. This can be very hard to do.

John found this out through much pain. "I always wanted my parents to accept Lenore but it never seemed to happen. They never did forgive me for getting divorced because they just loved my ex-wife. Well, they would ignore Lenore when we had conversations and would tell the kids to do the opposite of whatever she said. At first, Lenore and I argued constantly because I kept on sticking up for my parents. Eventually, I saw what was happening and confronted my parents. Of course they said it wasn't true but their denial seemed shallow to me. They were better for a while but things got back to being a hassle again. I just resolved myself to see them as little as possible and only do what I felt obligated to do. It's too bad it has to be this way but when I'm pushed to making a choice, I will always choose Lenore. I'd be a fool to not do that."

We think it is important that stepfamilies set relationships on their terms rather than living up to other's expectations. This does not mean that you abandon all your relatives, but rather that you have an "understanding" among your extended family. This understanding is based upon the assumption that you have some specific criteria for a continuing relationship:

- that relatives accept the family as it is
- that the past is less important than the present
- that you develop your memories right now rather than lament past moments
- that the new spouse is accepted as one of the family
- that the ex-spouse is not discussed unless "you" bring this person into a conversation.

Every relationship needs criteria to make it successful. Relatives can be a very supportive group if you let them know your needs. People hurt you because you are afraid to speak up. Strong relationships are enhanced by communication, not anger over unspoken words. We believe it is better to discuss painful issues rather than to run around them.

Traditional holidays for families may also be a tough problem. Usually, these are elaborated and stated in the divorce decree. If they are not explicit, we recommend that biological parents sit down and discuss how holidays will be spent and organized. We do not have any specific criteria except that the agreement be fair and that the children feel good about it. We attempt to guide families to celebrate two Christmases or two Thanksgivings if the children are to be gone for that specific day. Thus, memories for the stepfamily can also be created.

4. <u>Society</u>--We know that the stepfamily has trouble finding a niche in our culture. Even though one out of two marriages end in divorce and there are millions of individuals involved in stepfamilies, the place of the stepfamily is still uncertain.

This lack of identification tends to make you feel unwanted, out of place, angry, and sometimes even depressed. You may even have trouble introducing your children, your spouses, and your unique situation to others.

We have found no easy solution to dealing with our culture. It is your job, as stepfamily members, to tell people about your lives, both negative and positive. Too often people are complainers, and this leads to distorted perceptions on the part of others. You need to stand up for your rights and, if you are treated as an inferior person, speak up. No one will stand up for you if you don't. This certainly is an old adage but it works!

As a final note, it is important that stepfamilies reach out and help each other. Many people think that we are crazy for being in a stepfamily and wonder if we are going to make it. It is scary being out there all alone, not knowing if you can survive. Sometimes everyone seems against you and another person in a similar situation can be very helpful. When you meet people from a stepfamily, sit down and share with them. In therapy, we often use successful couples and families to help others. Sometimes the message seems clearer when it's not from a "professional" but from a peer. Stepfamilies have some unique struggles, difficulties, frustrations, joys, and accomplishments. Share your growth with others.

Creating Your Own Future
in the Future

In previous chapters we have shared many methods, techniques, and observations that can be helpful to a stepfamily. We have focused on both values and ingredients that can help you survive emotional difficulties. When you are in a stepfamily that seems in turmoil, it's hard to see beyond your immediate problem. It's important to shape your plans so that they affect both your present and your future.

The developmental process of stepfamilies takes many steps and variations. Looking at these steps can be helpful and may give you a perspective of what the future holds in store for you.

0-1 Month: This is both a time of havoc and of excitement for the stepfamily. The married couple is still on the "high" of romance while the children may be quite uncertain about what is going to occur. Many times the family is disrupted and everyone doesn't know how each person fits in the family. There can be lots of feelings shared which can hurt and yet set the stage for greater change. If the parents appear as if they do not know what they are doing, you may have a sinking ship. This is a time for listening and also some structure. People may not know what to call each other and limits must be set on what types of behavior are acceptable and which ones are not okay. Each person may seek a private space for retreat and this should be honored.

Expect a lot of tears, anger, discouragement, and moments of happiness during this time frame. It's important that the husband and wife stick together and not fight or argue in front of the children. Unresolved feelings toward ex-husbands and ex-wives may be very evident in the remarriage.

Mary and George felt both the pain and excitement that accompanied their remarriage. Both experienced a painful divorce as they were the ones that were "left behind." Both had custody of their children with George having two teenage sons and Mary bringing her 10- and 11-year-old daughters into the new family. Nothing seemed very easy for George and Mary even during their courtship period. Each expected the other person to make up for all the ex-husband's or ex-wife's mistakes. This was evident in two themes they kept expressing to each other. George to Mary: "never look at another man;" Mary to George: "don't work overtime because you're a workaholic."

The kids seemed to hassle them endlessly as they loved to join the battle. They fought with each other constantly as each person in the family determined who would dominate. They attempted to make Mary and George as unhappy as possible and they usually succeeded.

It wasn't too long after their remarriage that Mary and George thought about calling it quits. However, like most people who are pushed in a corner, they decided to try something different. They began to act as if nothing would break their marriage apart. Mary and George didn't fight in front of the kids and they set down reasonable rules of conduct and courtesy that all had to observe. Even if the kids were determined to make life miserable for them, George and Mary wouldn't let them know it. It wasn't exactly the way George and Mary planned it but it seemed to work.

<u>2-4 Months</u>: Life begins to settle down somewhat but the children may become more vocal and demand certain rights. There is still a feeling of uneasiness in regard to showing caring for family members and the new step-parent may be confused as to roles and function. This is an important time to reach out and to try to make the unit a stronger family. Sharing activities and helping people spend time together is very important.

The couple may feel that some of their freedoms have been taken away and must come to terms with vocational and home duties. If this is an area of conflict, the other family members may feed on it. Presenting an image of security is important even if the relationship is shaky at times. The children may still try to split up the marital relationship if they believe it would be better for them. The adults must lead the family during these early times and model appropriate caring and consideration for family members. Encouragement and support are prime characteristics of success during this time frame. If there were one word to describe this period, it would be "chaos."

Len, an electrician, has tried to forget this crazy period. "Joy and I were so much in love that we forgot to talk about how the house would be run. I just assumed that she would be like my ex-wife but boy was I about to receive a big surprise! Joy thought that we should share household duties and I had trouble understanding her point of view. I worked all hours of the day or night and I didn't feel like coming home and vacuuming. It wasn't too long before the kids got into the act. My teenage son said he didn't want to do it either because I didn't help and he wouldn't do 'woman's work.' Well, before I knew it the whole house was in an uproar and nothing seemed to be going right. In the end, I started to see her point of view and we all started doing chores together. It's not the most enjoyable thing in life but we seem a lot closer now."

<u>5-7 Months</u>: This can be a very up-and-down period for the stepfamily. If marital problems are occurring, they can reach a critical point during this period. The honeymoon is past and the realities of marriage sometimes force couples to reevaluate their decision about marriage and determine if it is going to work. On the other hand, seeking closeness and establishing ties can now occur. Many of the games that the family has been playing with each other are now understood and it is up to each family member to break through facades and attempt to get close. If family roles are uncertain, they must be more clearly defined. At times the family seems like it is going along with regularity and suddenly a

problem may appear. Children are still not quite ready to accept the situation as it is and may complain <u>but</u> less frequently than before.

This can be a tough time for the new parents. If they care for the child, the new mom or dad has probably been working very hard to get close to the child. And yet sometimes the relationship is not quite as good as the new parent wants. "I used to hate to hear the phone ring on Sunday mornings," Linda revealed. "Julie would get so excited talking to her mom and I really resented it. I did all the work and she never talked to me like that. I talked about it to Glenn but he didn't understand how I felt. I guess it was something that I have been working out myself. I know that Julie cares for me, but it's tough to compete with an idol. She's made her mother bigger than life. I guess that makes it better for her to cope with it but Glenn sometimes plays this game, too. If everything was so great, why did the two of them leave? When I bring it up to Glenn, he gets real defensive. Maybe I just want him to talk to Joy the same way about me as he does about her."

<u>8-12 Months</u>: A sense of pattern and stability should now be occurring. The children may be willing to show more affection if this is modeled. By this time, the new parent can be both better understood and integrated into the family. Family rules may still be misunderstood and expectations between child and parent will differ. It is the beginning foundation which should be in place by this time and if there are cracks, it will show. If therapy is needed, it will be very evident during this time period.

We have found that many families come to therapy during this time period because they have exhausted all possibilities and have nowhere else to go. Usually, they have missed many of the important first steps for beginning a healthy stepfamily and problems have piled up to where they are at a crisis level. At this point, we actually work at helping the family start anew. It's important to initiate steps and establish rules that will enhance interaction and understanding in the family. For instance, if the children or a new parent are refusing to get involved with each other, we discuss openly with the whole family the reasons this is occurring.

It is our belief that family members need to care for each other or else it's not a family but rather a collection of individuals who happen to live in the same house. Most often people in stepfamilies want to be close but do not know how to do it. So instead of helping each other, they may feel misunderstood and hurt.

13-18 Months: It is during this period that the family may begin to make sense. If ambivalent feelings are present on the part of the children or a parent, this will be a detriment to the family. Adults with inadequate parenting skills due to lack of experience will feel more comfortable during this time. The art of compromise and negotiations must be well learned by now or the marriage and the family will probably dissolve. Knowing that a second marriage might fail can be a motivator at this time if things are not going right. If the family is comfortable, most problems that appeared to be of crisis proportion six months ago seem much easier now. Decisions that are made may not please everybody, but that is one of the dilemmas of all families.

This is a point that many couples and families have trouble understanding. Any decision that a person makes tends to cause conflict. If there were no conflict, the decision would be too easy.

Thus, we see conflict as a part of every family. The problem is often how we deal with conflict rather than the conflict itself. As families grow older, some conflicts are inevitable. Children become teenagers, a newborn arrives, a child leaves home, a grandparent dies, and many more such occurrences happen in the life of a family. Since stepfamily members sometimes feel unsure about themselves and their role in the family, a conflict can easily become a crisis. If this occurs then counseling is usually a necessary help.

Ralph and Judy would be an example of a conflict that grew into a crisis. Having been married five years, neither of them could ever agree on parenting. This conflict was glossed over until their son Timmy became a teenager. Ralph thought he needed to be let free and grow up as he, Ralph, did. Therefore, he didn't find anything wrong with Timmy staying out to three or four in the morning driving the car step-Dad just bought him. Judy thought otherwise and believed Timmy should be at home studying. With each event, they continued to fight and argue while Timmy was stuck in the middle. Eventually, Timmy messed up and was arrested for drunk driving. Ralph and Judy fought until Ralph lost his temper and he hit Judy. She then left the house and sought family counseling as a help for their problem.

<u>19-24 Months</u>: We anticipate that it takes approximately two years for the stepfamily to reach some state of normalcy. By this time period, most painful losses have been assimilated and, hopefully, life appears more positive. Most stepfamilies realize by this time that they are different and not re-created nuclear families.

Honesty is a core ingredient of the family unit. By this time, the foundation has been laid where individuals understand each other and can give the amount of caring that is both comfortable and positive. The pitfalls are visible and can be hopped over rather than falling in and complaining.

Sometimes decisions made in the stepfamily can be painful. For instance, Mary's teenage son named Ted would run off to his Dad's house whenever he didn't get what he wanted or was disciplined. His attitude was "I'll show you if you don't let me do what I want." His relationship with his Dad was good, but Ted didn't like any restrictions being placed on him. Mary and her ex-husband talked about the problem and worked out a solution where Ted would be allowed to visit almost any time except when there was a disagreement at home. This continued for several years until Ted reached 16 years of age. At that time, he requested to move in with his father. Since his Dad had not remarried, Ted received more attention and monetary rewards with his father than in his stepfamily. Painfully, Mary let Ted leave and he seemed happy for a while. However, his father had to discipline him also and eventually his Dad remarried.

We admit that the nature of the stepfamily can lead to disorganization. Many people do not know what to do or are confronted with roles and situations for which they were never trained. Being a child is harder when you don't know in what setting you are supposed to be a child and to whom you can act like a child. Maybe you're used to acting like an adult in the family and you don't wish to give up that role when Mom or Dad remarry.

Adults can have similar feelings. They may resent not being close to some of "their" children and too close to others. Expecting to love someone immediately can be a large task for anyone. Trying to be a parent when no one treats you "like" a parent can also be tough. These are roles that are supposedly reserved for biological partners and no one else is allowed to practice them. We believe this is a myth that is no more true than saying that love is a limited commodity. With both the rate of divorce and remarriage rising at the present level, people have no choice but to think, act, and feel differently about the stepfamily.

Our belief is that people can sit around and moan or complain about their marriages and families as they fall apart or take the initiative to make them work. In all honesty, there are going to be few people who will jump up and say, "Isn't it terrific that you have a stepfamily. I'm so proud of you!" More likely it will be, "Oh, a stepfamily. Is that like a real family?"

You must remember that divorce in America has only become a reality for most people during the last several decades. Though we agree that divorce is a devastating experience for most of us, the process of ending and beginning relationships has changed in America. Whether it is good or bad, people are staying in relationships because it is a positive growth experience for them and not "for the children" or for everyone else. National statistics don't lie, and they present a very interesting picture for American families. The national divorce rate has quadrupled during the past 50 years, while the average family size has shrunk. Three out of four divorced women and five out of six divorced men eventually remarry, many within three years of their divorce. In 1982, the median age for second marriages dropped again to approximately 31 years of age for women and 35 years for men. Many people are getting out of marriages while they are still young and hope that the second time will be more successful.

People in America are beginning to believe that intimate relationships and family can be one of the most exciting aspects of life or one of the most devastating. Too many individuals are unwilling to be psychologically, emotionally, or physically abused for the sake of society. The converse is also true. In a culture where everything is super stimulating, people expect marriage to be like Atari video games. If it is only "fair," you may want to bail out and find the perfect person. If this is true, the stepfamily usually knows these individuals out of their fantasy life.

Most folks have an idea about what a stepfamily entails but few of the realities. They expect it to be like a biological family, and then easily give up if it isn't. While they may be alike, it is also true that the stepfamily requires many roles for which the traditional family has no explanation. But it is a family, and it does have some of the following characteristics you may want to keep in mind when times get hard:

1. You have a marriage. A spouse that cares for you and is doing the best that he or she can.

2. You are a parent. No matter what anyone says, you still are parenting children in your house and possibly out of the home.

3. Children can respect and learn to love you. Everyone can be loved and is loveable. Always, it takes effort and time.

4. You have a life apart from your children just like all good marriages. Don't dedicate your entire life to your kids. Some day you'll be disappointed. They usually grow up and leave.

5. You can have a caring and nurturing environment. This is what family means. A place where you are accepted for what you are.

6. Your kids can have activities and a life that you can both support and in which you can become involved. Good parents take time out to be with their kids alone and together.

7. You can have special memories and experiences. A stepfamily has more than its share of ups and downs. These can make the family very strong. Often, families that go through hardship come out stronger in the end. As you progress, learn to laugh at the "old days" rather than keeping past resentments.

8. You can become a better spouse and parent as time goes on. Give yourself a break once in a while. Nobody's perfect and we all make mistakes. Thomas Jefferson said that if he made a mistake only once, he would be a smart man. Everyone needs experience.

9. As time goes on, a family gets better. Learn to compromise and live with each other. Time can be a healer of wounds and it can also satisfy a family.

10. Remember that through it all, you're okay. Don't give up on yourself and your ability to make life what you want it to be. The moment you stop believing in yourself, the family will also have trouble. Success in anything demands hard work and perseverance.

Another important point that requires further elaboration is that stepfamilies can have their own children just like other families. Many times a couple in a family will have a child of their own. Sometimes this causes them to be married. At other times it may be an accident or it may be a planned event. No matter what the case, adding a child can have a dramatic impact on the stepfamily. Generally, it can either be a strongly positive or hazardous experience.

If a couple decides to have a child to keep their marriage or their family together, it most likely will do the opposite. Whatever troubles the couple or family were having will become accentuated because of the baby. For instance, Mary wanted to have a child because Sam wasn't around very much and stayed at work. When they were together it was usually a miserable experience. After the baby was born, Sam did stay around for a month or two. However, he and Mary continually fought and so he retreated back to working every night. Because the baby needed more attention and more of Mary's time, she resented Sam being gone. Their fights became horrendous. Even the baby would receive the brunt of their anger if the child cried or misbehaved. Eventually, Mary and Sam left the marriage in utter chaos, both angry at each other and the child. Sometimes having a child slowly deteriorates a relationship if the couple is not prepared for the experience.

On a positive note, a newborn child can also bring a family together. The baby can be a strong binding force between the couple and can certainly be a joyous and beautiful experience; if they are willing to work together and share responsibilities concerning the child, it can be very good for a marriage. In the stepfamily, it can also help bring all the children together. Sometimes, it makes all family members feel more like a family because of the new child. Everyone has something in common and much to talk about and share. A new baby can be a uniting force if the family is ready.

It's important to remember that creating a family takes time. Even though children may rebel and refuse to accept a parent in a "stepfamily," they eventually realize that being part of a family is a strong need for most of us. Family gives us a sense of security, caring, and acceptance that the "outside world" often does not fulfill. A strong couple passes on behaviors, values, norms, and attitudes to their children not "biologically" but rather through the sharing of time, experience, and life. Stepfamilies can create a lot of happiness for the individuals involved in this situation. The work may be harder, but the rewards can be great.